COPING WITH HIS SUCCESS

Coping with His Success

A SURVIVAL GUIDE FOR WIVES

Frances Bremer and Emily Vogl

HARPER & ROW, PUBLISHERS, New York

Cambridge, Philadelphia, San Francisco, London
Mexico City, São Paulo, Sydney

1817

Grateful acknowledgment is made for permission to reprint:

"Are You Burning Out?" and excerpts from *Burn Out* by Dr. Herbert J. Freudenberger, Ph.D. Copyright © 1980 by Herbert J. Freudenberger, Ph.D. Reprinted by permission of Doubleday & Company, Inc.

Excerpts from Ann Landers' Column first appeared in *The Washington Post,* December 1982. Reprinted by permission of Ann Landers, Field Newspaper Syndicate and *The Washington Post.*

FIRST EDITION

Designer: Sidney Feinberg

Library of Congress Cataloging in Publication Data

Bremer, Frances Winfield.

Coping with his success.

Includes index.

1. Wives—United States—Social conditions.

2. Wives—United States—Psychology. 3. Success.

I. Vogl, Emily. II. Title.

HQ759.B759 1984   646.7′8   83-48330

ISBN 0-06-015247-8

---

84 85 86 87 88 10 9 8 7 6 5 4 3 2 1

To Jerry and Frank, our "Men at the Top,"
and to Leila, Paul and Marc

CONTENTS

ACKNOWLEDGMENTS

We would like to thank our families and friends for their tremendous patience and encouragement and all the women who took part in our research, without whom there would have been no book.

PREFACE

The idea for this book came from a telephone conversation between two good friends. Emily called Francie one afternoon with a cry for help. "Please don't go overseas again without telling me how to cope," she begged. Her husband, Frank, who had been a journalist for *The Times* of London for many years, had just taken a prestigious but demanding job at the World Bank. Francie's husband, Jerry, is a Foreign Service officer. The Bremers had lived on three continents in fifteen years with time in between in Washington, where Jerry had always held high-powered, high-pressured jobs. Francie considers herself one of the "lucky" ones, having been forced to come to terms early with the demands of her husband's career.

We decided to write a book about women with similar problems. Our original title came out of Emily's despair: *The Power Widows: Stress and Burnout in Wives at the Top.* It would be a book telling how miserable life was for these women, who appeared to have it all. It would also reveal how other women who are married to successful men view their marriages. What effect does a successful but frequently absent father have on children? Can a wife develop a career of her own if her husband's work is very demanding? Can she maintain her old friendships? What are her support systems? How does she deal with loneliness? How strong is her own identity? How does she cope and where does she get her strength from? As it turned out, there were also many good things to be said about being married to such men, and many of the women we interviewed dealt successfully with their problems and led happy and fulfilled married lives.

We mailed one thousand questionnaires to women across America. We wanted a cross section of women whose lives we thought would be heavily influenced by the high-pressure jobs of their husbands. So our mailing went to women whose husbands' names were drawn from lists of those prominent in politics, banking, industry, the law, civil service and journalism. The responses were tremendous. And as a result of early publicity about the book, we were deluged with mail from other women who also wanted to participate in our study but whose husbands' names were not on any lists, much less household words. These were the wives of doctors, lawyers, military men, public officials, self-employed businessmen, managers and farmers.

More than 150 women worked through the 65 questions of our questionnaire* and poured out their feelings, impressions and experiences. Most sought confidentiality, and so we have not identified them here.

Women responded from such cities as New York, San Francisco and Chicago, from such dissimilar states as Florida, Montana and Alaska and from military bases overseas. We conducted personal interviews with many of them. Our conclusions are based on the views of these women, women whose lives are directly and personally affected by the business of the White House, the Congress, the judiciary and the big board rooms of corporate America, and also women whose husbands have achieved their success without high visibility.

The average age of the women who participated in our study was forty-two. The average participant had been married for twenty years and had three or more children. She was a college graduate and did not have a career of her own. Most of our respondents, with the exception of those discussed in Chapter 3, were nonworking women, so our study is largely limited to this group. A survey of younger women might have produced different results, but it is our strong feeling that most of the problems we address in our book are shared by older and younger women, despite the fact that it may be easier

*A copy of the questionnaire is printed at the end of the book.

for younger women to face the issues and resolve them than it is for older women.

We also want to stress emphatically that men may be "at the top" no matter where they are or what they do; it is the energy and time commitment which take the toll, not the "job description" of the man. That is, if a man runs the local chamber of commerce in a small town, chairs the annual blood drive for the Red Cross and is on the local water committee and the school board, he can be just as involved as a man who is chairman of an international bank.

We have very little information about how men in these marriages feel, apart from what their wives told us. Obviously husbands and wives may differ greatly in their ability and desire to communicate. Views of marriage are subjective, and undoubtedly many of the husbands of the women we spoke with had very different views about their marriages from the ones their wives express in this book. But, however subjective, it is the views of the women, *their* frustrations, difficulties, joys and solutions, that we have sought to address.

A husband may feel deeply about his wife but not say so. Men and women may never be able to communicate perfectly. Yet the message that came through most clearly while we were doing our research was that there is a need for better communication and more open communication between husbands and wives. And there is almost as great a need for some degree of self-sufficiency on the part of *both* partners, so that one does not rely unrealistically on the other for intellectual stimulation or emotional support. We discuss the issue of self-sufficiency for women in the chapter on careers, but it also affects child raising, friendships and dealing with stresses. Ironically it appears to be those wives who have developed some kind of self-sufficiency who are also the best able to form a real team with their husbands.

Throughout the book we have often had to identify women simply as the wives of politicians, businessmen and so on. Although we would have preferred to avoid this altogether, we used so many short quotes from anonymous sources that it was impossible to create a persona for each woman quoted. Some women gave us permission to identify them as the authors of their quotes; those who did not, yet whom we have quoted extensively, have been given pseudonyms and any clues as to their identity have been changed. But there remain some who have been identified only in terms of their husbands' professions. We hope that the reader will understand that we don't consider these women merely extensions of their husbands but very much VIPs in their own right.

One last disclaimer is necessary. Neither of us is a professional pollster or psychologist. Our sample was too small to be conclusive. Our own educational backgrounds are in history and literature. But we know our subject at first hand, and we have talked to some wise and wonderful women who have shared many insights with us. Also we are committed to our marriages and to marriage as an institution. Throughout the book you will find guidelines pointing the way to coping successfully with special problems. If we can help just one woman in a similar situation find greater happiness in her marriage, it will have been worth the work.

F.B. and E.V.

Washington, D.C.

INTRODUCTION

Of the thousands of letters we received, one of the best came from a woman in Texas. She exemplifies the struggle of many other women in her position.

Dear Frances and Emily,

Your appearance on *The Phil Donahue Show* was aired in our area today. I think the reason you were given such a hostile and unfriendly reception was because you were from what would be considered by most to be the "upper crust" level. However, I could identify with what you were saying even though I'm in the middle working class. My husband is a classic workaholic, which I didn't know when we were married twenty-six years ago. That word wasn't used way back then. The traits that go with that type of personality were those that were most admired by all social standards: hard-working, responsibility, etc.

We were married in that period where everyone had an idea of who was supposed to be doing what as far as roles were concerned. It was understood from the beginning that I was to quit my job when the children came. The father goes to work, the mother stays home and raises the family. Which was fine with me. I never felt that my duties were second to my husband's in importance.

I was raised in the era that told women that it was their responsibility to make or break a successful marriage, the old "hand that rocks the cradle rules the world" bit. Society even condoned a man "going elsewhere" if he didn't get enough affection at home. Remember that one?

So we women had to work at being Super Women, which we tried because after all, with all that power we had to. In fact many times I felt sorry for my husband having to go outside the home to work. He had to deal with the orders from his boss and the whims of the customers, grouches and all. He had to leave the house while his three sons were still sleeping and sometimes didn't get home again until after they were back in bed for the night. He missed seeing their cute antics and first achievements; walking, paddy-cake, etc. I on the other hand could do my work in the comfortable surroundings of my home and neighborhood. I set my own schedule and could adjust it any time or way I liked. I thoroughly enjoyed raising my sons and being Queen Bee of our little kingdom. All was as it should be.

That's the way it was for seventeen years. The boys understood, through my training of course, that Daddy had to work hard to support us, so everything possible was geared to his comfort and ease when he was home. House and children had to be clean and quiet. We were ready at a minute's notice to do whatever he wished on a weekend. It was never expected that he would or could attend any school functions although by this time he (notice I didn't say "we") was in business for himself just two miles from home. Business always came first. Of course we understood this and accepted it, even though the children saw other fathers at these affairs.

As I said, all this worked for seventeen years. By then the boys were grown up enough to be involved in their school activities and friends, not to need Mama sitting at home with milk and cookies waiting for them. I now had time to reflect, at thirty-five years of age, on what the future was going to hold for me.

I had always helped my husband with the business, at least part of it. He would bring home the paper work, which he didn't care to do, and I would do it; payroll, accounts payable and receivable, etc. I had no part in policy or decision making; that was his alone.

By the time I tried to discuss with him what I thought should start our next phase or stage of life, I was shocked to find out that he didn't share my concern at all. After all, he still had his business to attend to as always. He felt no need to change anything. I had thought once we raised the boys to near adulthood and provided for their education we could start to relax and enjoy our lives together a bit more. But I found out he expected me to go along as always even if I didn't have any job of my own.

He didn't much care what I did with my time and energy as long as it didn't interfere with his work. No, he didn't want me working at his business nor taking an outside job. His pride would be crushed if, in the wording of the Dark Ages, "his woman would have to bring home the money." It would be ok if I wanted to do volunteer work somewhere (which I, like so many other women, had been doing right along with raising the children). I could do anything I wanted to as long as I didn't get paid for it or it interfered with the housework or meal schedule. Talk about freedom, WOW!

When I tried to point out what I really wanted was more of my husband, to be back in step with him and spend more time together, the answer was always the same, "How much more can I do, how many hours do you want me to work?" Of course this would make me feel guilty. I spent the next three years feeling unworthy of love from anyone, even my boys, relatives, friends, neighbors, anyone.

Here I was, this very selfish woman with a nice home, car, three really fine sons, and a hard working husband who brought home his money, didn't drink or beat his family; a man who was always ready and willing to help his neighbors. Could any normal woman want any more???

To all outward appearances we were perfect. Emotions were never talked about. If a woman felt anything, it was put down to being "that time of month" or, after a certain age, "must be the change coming on." Talk about a no-win situation, that's it. We had three rotten years where we fought, something we hadn't done in the first seventeen years. I (pardon me) ASKED him for a divorce, after which he let me know I would get nothing because I had never earned anything outside. I was so dumb that I believed it. I even considered suicide a couple of times but gave up because 1) I didn't want my sons to feel they might somehow be defective too if they had a crazy mother, and 2) I feared God himself would disapprove of my selfishness.

I took up drinking in a small way but developed ulcers. Meanwhile everyone around us was feeling sorry for my husband because he had to not only work so hard but had to also put up with this crazy woman. I felt like my only function in life now was to be a wart on my husband's elbow, just a little something not worth noticing all the time but an annoyance now and then.

As I got closer to the time when all my boys would be gone and I would be turning forty years old, I started thinking things out more clearly without panic and realized that I never would be able to keep up with my husband's idea of what I should be and that I damn well better get thinking of what I wanted to become for myself. I sure didn't care for me the way I was. Certainly not the type of woman I'd ever want my sons to marry.

I am now forty-five and on my way. I've set goals and let everyone know, my husband and everyone else who ever had an opinion on what I was supposed to be, that the next ten, fifteen, or twenty years are going to be mine. Sink or swim, I will grow, expand, take time for my friends and interests. Anyone who wants to walk along with me, I'll be glad of their company, but it will be in my direction.

Of course my husband tells everyone that I am one of "those women's libbers" but name calling doesn't faze me. I still do all the paper work for the business but I no longer get the ulcer when he complains about business matters. I listen and nod because I know he doesn't really want any opinions or suggestions. It is his business and always will be. I had told him years ago it was awfully crowded sleeping in our bed with all those creditors and customers in between us, so we reached an agreement that we would not have any discussion of business affairs in the bedroom. Oh, the sweet taste of victory.

I still keep a reasonably clean house, cook nutritious meals because that is a value of mine. In general the only things that have changed are that he has stopped treating me like a retarded child and he doesn't put me down when I state my side of things.

I am now enrolled in classes which I hope will lead me to a career of my own within the next five years, which I hope to keep for at least ten to twenty-five years, so when I do get to the retirement stage I will not be at that terribly dependent level I was at twenty-seven years ago. The past is dead, may it never rise again.

Recently my sons, who are now twenty-four, twenty-two, and

twenty, told me how proud they are of me now that I have finally started to grow up like I helped them to. They even offer to help me with my homework! That is the most rewarding aspect of my entire adult life. I have raised three males that will find a better balance of work and family and emotional stability than they saw with their parents.

There is a whole army of these men out there on every level. The disease of being a workaholic is not confined to any level or price range. I know now that those traits are not virtues but can be vices if they exclude personal relationships or family.

SUE SMITH*
Texas

*Not her real name.

With the exception of certain prominent individuals, the names, characteristics, backgrounds and other details about the people described in this book have been changed.

COPING WITH HIS SUCCESS

1

MARRIAGE

Fernand and Anne Spaak appeared to all who met them on the Washington diplomatic circuit to be an extraordinarily successful couple. She was charmingly outspoken, and he seemed destined for still more success, having already been made ambassador to the United States for the European Communities. But those who knew the Spaaks well realized that their marriage was filled with tensions and that the harmonious outward appearance was no more than a façade.

Nobody was surprised when Spaak left Washington for a top post in Brussels, but even old friends of the Spaaks were shocked when they opened The *New York Times* on July 20, 1981, and read: "Fernand Spaak, chief aid to the President of the Common Market and a member of one of Belgium's most influential political families, was shot to death by his wife, who then electrocuted herself in the bathtub of their apartment in Brussels."

Only a few years earlier, when the Spaaks had been in the United States for six months, Anne had been featured in another *New York Times* article. An attractive, intelligent woman in her fifties, she was called "a diplomat's wife with a difference." She had already traveled widely in this country and had broken out of the mold. Rather than being relegated to the small talk of receiving lines or taking her place at the ladies' luncheon tables, she was speaking to groups on the status of European women.

She had never made a speech in her life before coming to America, but here her first impression was that everyone did something.

"I didn't meet a woman who wasn't involved in a job or some kind of volunteer work," she said. So she decided to accompany her husband when he traveled around the United States lecturing on the European Common Market, establishing her own speaking schedule.

Anne's devotion to a united Europe dated back to her work with the Belgian Resistance during the war. Half Belgian, half Italian, she was passionately anti-Nazi. After the war she was awarded the Belgian Croix de Guerre for having blown up a German arms depot when she was eighteen. Nothing else in her life ever measured up to this heroic deed.

As the wife of Fernand Spaak—himself the wealthy son of a founder of the European Communities—she lived in Brussels and Luxembourg, raising six children but "never really doing anything with my life." When she came to America, she was determined to change this.

The Spaaks lived in an elegant mansion on Belmont Road in Washington. The house, with its Spanish façade, French and English furniture and Italian cook, seemed to reflect the Europeanness of the Spaaks. Indeed Anne described herself as a citizen of Europe rather than of any one country.

At their large and frequent dinner parties they entertained politicians and diplomats from both sides of the Atlantic. They were extremely popular, and invitations for cocktails and dinner poured in. Their travel schedule also demanded a great deal of time, but Anne thrived on the travel and said later that her four years in America were "the happiest years of my life."

Anne Spaak had finally found a purpose in her life. She loved people, she loved to travel, and she responded wholeheartedly to American warmth and hospitality. She became a very effective speaker. Enthusiastic about her life here, she was also proud that she could appear beside the husband she adored.

Fernand Spaak was charming but extremely egotistical and given to violent outbursts. However, his good looks and distinguished manners made him well liked wherever he went, especially by women. Unfortunately Fernand did not understand the change in his wife since coming to the United States and seemed to resent her efforts to develop as a person in her own right. He allowed her to travel with him but mocked her new-found enthusiasms. The more she changed, the more hostile toward her he became. Often he rejected her sexually too, not even bothering to hide his extramarital affairs from her.

But Anne never stopped loving him and never openly acknowledged their problems. Finally, putting aside her hopes for more independence, she decided to try to win back his affection in the old way. She bought a new dress for a ball her husband was giving. She made a special trip to New York to find an evening gown that would really stun him. She hoped she would get at least a comment from him if not a compliment. But he paid no attention to her the whole evening. Finally, as they were getting ready for bed, she asked him whether he had liked her dress, and confessed that it had cost eight thousand dollars. Drunk and enraged, he screamed at her, loud enough for the servants cleaning up downstairs to hear, "I'll show you who is going to pay for it!" and tore the dress off her in shreds.

When she realized that there was no longer any hope for her marriage, Anne made plans to remain in Washington after Fernand's tour of duty ended the following year. But Fernand refused to support her financially if she stayed behind. Anne's dream of a new life here gradually faded, and she finally agreed to return to Belgium with him. She knew then that things would never really change for her.

Shortly after resuming his duties in Brussels, Fernand moved in with his latest mistress and left Anne alone. Her children were grown and didn't need her. She had no husband, no skills and therefore no future, she felt. In desperation she killed him and then herself.

The Spaaks' case is a tragic one, but some of their problems are not unique. Many wives leading lives that are the envy of others sometimes feel miserable, if not murderous. In this chapter we will look at other marriages, some successful, some not, and examine the special problems wives of successful men have to face. We will see how a man's drive to succeed and the rise to power can put strains on a relationship.

We will begin by looking at the backgrounds of the women who marry these men. Did they have happy childhoods? Why did they marry their husbands? Did they know what they were letting themselves in for? And how do they rate their own marriages?

Great Expectations

Sixty percent of the women we surveyed said that they had had happy childhoods. The vast majority of these answered the question with a simple yes. Twenty-five percent rated their childhoods as only moderately happy, and 15 percent said they had had unhappy childhoods. Some went into great detail on the subject. Although we did not find a strong connection between happy childhoods and happy marriages, or the reverse, we felt that the answers to this question were important in forming a total picture of these women and their lives.

Roscoe Dellums, the wife of a California congressman, and the second of six girls, told us that her childhood had a marked effect on the way she views her life now:

> *My grandmother, Esther Jones Lee, had been appointed by the then governor of California, Earl Warren, to sit on the Republican Central Committee, so there was always politics in our family. She used to stage one-woman pickets around the state capitol to protest segregated accommodations.*
>
> *Sometimes she would gather us little kids together, dress us up and take us with her to a restaurant. They wouldn't serve us because we were black. Then my grandmother would call Governor Warren, and he would come down in his limousine and shock everybody.*
>
> *We learned at an early age that you can do something for social justice. We all felt we had a mission in life beyond our personal gratification. There are things you have to do for family, there are things you have to do for community and things you have to do for the country.*

Other women spoke of a feeling of being loved and well cared for. Some mentioned financial security as an important part of their past, but not all the women we questioned came from affluent backgrounds. Many were middle and lower class but enjoyed solid educations and close family ties.

Many spoke of a great deal of positive reinforcement and a feeling of family togetherness which still existed. The happily married wife of a successful lawyer said that her parents' greatest gift to her was making her feel that she could do anything she wanted to and succeed.

Maria, the dark, vivacious wife of a diplomat, who herself once worked for the State Department, felt well prepared for living overseas because her parents had immigrated to the United States just before she was born. She added:

> *My sister used to tease me because she was born in Europe, which was much more exotic and romantic than being born in Chicago. I did go to Europe when I was fifteen and learned another language. It gave me a taste for European life, which has certainly made a career in the Foreign Service easier.*

Sarah, an artist and the wife of a CIA agent, though she grew up in an impoverished environment, saw an interesting parallel between her childhood and that of their own children:

> *I had a reasonably happy, stable family life with two strict Catholic parents. I had an older sister, which made me "try harder." My father was a shift worker, and I remember not seeing him as much as I needed to. Now I see the same thing happening to our sons and their father.*

Older women often grew up in economically hard times, and this naturally affected their childhoods. Angela is the mother of three and the wife of an oil tycoon. She asked us:

> *What is a happy childhood? I grew up in the Depression, when money was tight and there was plenty of pain and sorrow. But so is there in all growing up.*

Another woman of the same age agreed:

> *My childhood was marked by family deterioration, severe economic troubles, isolation and alienation from society.*

Obviously the times that these women grew up in strongly marked their characters.

Liza, the daughter of immigrants who is now married to a government official, also had a difficult childhood but for different reasons:

Childhood was a painful time for me. I didn't want to be different, nobody does when she's young. I had braids and rode a bike while the other teenagers wore pedal pushers and rode around in convertibles.

Alcoholism in the family was mentioned by several women as a real problem. One spoke of her father as a "nonviolent alcoholic." Another told us that her father was laid off because of drinking and she was frightened to death most of the time. And this thought-provoking answer came from the wife of a Midwestern businessman:

My father was a periodic alcoholic, the kind who didn't drink every day. He would drink on the holidays, and once he started, he couldn't stop. All during my childhood he was drinking like this periodically. Every holiday was ruined, Thanksgiving, Christmas, the Fourth of July.

But in spite of this I don't think of my childhood as unhappy. I used to be very bitter towards him because I thought, if he really cared for us, why would he do this to us?

But if I'm a strong person today, I guess that's what made me strong. I had to be strong to survive.

An airline pilot's wife saw a definite connection between how she was raised as a child and the kind of man she wanted to marry:

My mother was an actress, and my father was in advertising. Actually he was a writer. I was an only child, and they were older parents. I was born when they were in their forties, so I was a child adult, groomed for success.

If I took piano lessons, I was going to play in Carnegie Hall; if I wrote a story in the second grade, it was going to be a best seller. Naturally, being the little brat that I was, I thought, "Why can't they just leave me alone?"

I guess what attracted me most to my husband was that he had a really strong sense of himself, and I didn't. I was trying to live up to my parents' sense of me. He had a strong sense of himself early without being an egomaniac, although I think he has become that in later years.

These women married their husbands for many of the same reasons that most women marry. Love, physical attraction, timing, common backgrounds, pregnancy and the desire to escape from home or the sorority house were all factors cited. Louise, who grew up in the South, suggested that for her, marriage was not only expected but it was her "manifest destiny" and that she would be considered a failure if she didn't marry.

Several younger women told us that they hadn't planned to marry before establishing a career of their own but that they had been swept off their feet. "Couldn't bear not to," said a publisher's wife.

The qualities they loved in their husbands were: competence; tenderness; intelligence; humor; vitality; and "a sense of command which gave me the feeling that if he was there, everything would always be all right."

For many it was not a case of love at first sight. A teacher from St. Louis, married to a department store manager, told us:

I was twenty-four when he asked me. I had just come out of a bad relationship. He was nice, handsome and established in his own business. He called constantly, sent me flowers too. One week after we met, he proposed.

I was taken aback and had to think. I knew I didn't love him enough to marry him, but most of my friends were married and I felt he had all the things I liked. I felt my love would grow. It did.

Maria told us that she really didn't like her husband when they first met, ironically for some of the same reasons which led to his success:

When I first met him, I really didn't like him. He was so "antsy." It was as if there was always an emergency. He never took the elevator at work. He was always running up the stairs, at the embassy. I used to think, "My God, did they declare war?"

It was six or eight months before we really talked. My father was a lot like him. He's a very driven man too, very successful in what he did.

My father never owned a pair of slippers because he never had time to put them on. Consciously I wasn't looking for that kind of man.

That's why I didn't like Tony in the beginning. I thought, "Do I need this again?" It wasn't until I got to know him better that I discovered that he had a lot of qualities that were compatible with my life interests, and then the antsy business started to take a back seat.

Shirley, a nurse who is married to a government official, felt that her husband had outgrown her in many ways but believed that originally he picked her out to fit in with his future dreams.

We were both from the Southwest. I think he was very impressed with me at the time. I had just returned from a summer as an exchange student. I came from a small city, but he was a country boy, and I had a level of sophistication that he didn't have, especially compared to the girls he had gone to school with.

But I don't think I "wow" him anymore. He is very critical now.

A successful career woman chose a man who wasn't threatened by her own need to succeed. "I'm as much of a workaholic as he is, and it's still a mutually cooperative arrangement," she said. Audrey, a psychologist, found a man who was intelligent and challenging. "I wanted someone who was as strong and bright as I was," she admitted frankly. And Karen, a Foreign Service wife, was forced to marry her boyfriend because they were posted overseas and the embassy wouldn't allow "live-ins."

Phyllis, a Massachusetts professor's wife who described her own childhood as desperately unhappy—"If I had it to live over again, I would rather not be born at all"—is married to an understanding and compassionate man who puts as high a value on a happy marriage as she does:

*I loved him dearly then and still do. I feel the greatest blessing
on earth is a good marriage. After my miserable childhood I am
all the more appreciative.*

Down to Earth

Many women married men with whom they shared common interests and goals. The ideal of working together is a very appealing one, although after marriage the reality is often different from the expectation.

Jennifer, who had stopped working since her marriage to a politician, told us that she really hadn't known what she was getting into:

*I was a lobbyist, and since we were both social activists, our
intentions were to get married and work together on the issues we
both care about. I wanted to continue to dovetail our work, but I
found out that when he says we can work together, it means I can
stand next to him in the receiving line and shake hands.*

Sarah also spoke of disillusionment:

*The first time I met Bruce, I knew he would be my husband.
We had similar interests and ideals. He was bright and masculine
but also very gentle and caring. He was open too and very communicative.*

*Then the CIA reinforced their old rules of being secretive and
closemouthed and he became like a robot; wind him up and he
talks, wind him up and he walks, but he can never speak for
himself. He keeps this attitude towards everyone, even his family.*

Did these women know what they were getting into? Did they consciously marry a man headed for success? Most told us that although they were attracted to "doers," they were quite unprepared for what life with such a man might bring.

One young woman, not yet married, argued that "before anybody gets married, they should know what they're in for." Many women maintained that this was impossible. But the wife of the CEO of a multinational corporation felt that she had gotten just what she had wanted, with no surprises and few regrets.

It's marvelous being associated with a man who is intelligent and vibrant and moves in interesting circles. It takes a special kind of female to ride with this kind of man, one who can take charge of the life she has chosen to lead.

I purposely chose to marry this man somewhat aware of what the future would be. When he sorrowfully, guiltily talks about the little time he has for the children, I try to allow him to see himself as the pioneer leaving his family in the covered wagon alone so he can go off and hunt or fight the Indians.

I have very little sympathy for the child-wife who cannot operate her home and live like an adult.

Rating a Marriage

We asked our respondents to rate their marriages at the time of filling out the questionnaire or of being interviewed. We felt that this was one of the most important items on the questionnaire and found that it had a very interesting tie-in with a later question, "What would you do if he left you tomorrow?"

Sixty-five percent of the women rated their marriages from good to excellent, while 35 percent felt that theirs were below average. Because each woman is unique and each marriage unique, it is obviously impossible for us to analyze their responses scientifically. But it is clear that one person's heaven is another's hell. For example, Angela, who rated her marriage "excellent," went on to say, "He's totally wrapped up in his job, and so is everyone else in the family." Another woman might have rated this marriage "miserable."

As society changes, so do our expectations of marriage. The traditional, hierarchical marriage of their grandmothers would be unacceptable to most young wives today. But do higher expectations make for happier marriages? In general we found that the older women we questioned rated their marriages higher than the younger ones did. Perhaps this was because life was less stressful for the women who had reached their fifties or sixties. They had more time for themselves and more time to spend with their husbands. They were less conflicted between marriage and motherhood. Perhaps they also didn't expect as much from marriage as the younger women did and had settled for less. And women of all ages told us that their marriages were much better than "many around that are falling apart." There was a great deal of pride in just keeping a marriage together at all in a time of ever-rising divorce rates.

One of the most thoughtful answers to the question "How do you rate your marriage now?" came from Eleanor, a forty-eight-year-old mother of two who had chosen to give up a career in publishing when she married her banker husband:

Our marriage of twenty years is very solid, very workable insofar as most matters are concerned, but not as good as it might be in terms of our relationship, communication, emotion, etc.

I say solid because we are both firmly committed to the marriage. It is a help to both of us to regard it as sacramental and irrevocable. But even without that I think we would each be deeply committed to it. My husband is a firm believer in contracts and commitments. My own childhood was so adversely affected by my mother's several divorces. We both feel it is far better to work out our differences than to give up.

I say workable because logistically and philosophically it goes fairly smoothly. He leaves the family banking to me, so we never have disputes over money. We do not fight about politics or religion (though we used to disagree on this). Housekeeping and related matters work out to his satisfaction. We trust each other completely, so that there is never any worry about extraneous relationships.

With so much going for us, we ought to have a more satisfying relationship than we do. His attitude is that there is nothing wrong with our marriage; he's happy with it just the way it is. I often think that I should count my blessings and be satisfied. But I do believe it could be a lot better if there were more communication between us. I think he thinks he is protecting me by not relating his problems and woes. He expects me to do the same for him.

But I often need to share problems and work them out with his help, and I don't like his putting me off or his refusal to consider that my emotional needs are valid. I think that in protecting me from problems he also protects himself from me.

I think he does not desire the openness I feel I need. I feel we need more unanimity in our relationship too. We are really most often at odds, pulling in different directions rather than working together, and for this we need positive communication.

What we have ranges from negative to nil, nothing gets said unless it is to complain. But he is unresponsive even to my efforts to discuss things like this, considering me quarrelsome if I try to raise such matters with him.

As he came to understand how much he was missing by avoiding the children, I think he may eventually come to the same realization where I am concerned. At least I hope he will; my turn next!

Many of the positive and negative elements in Eleanor's marriage were mentioned by other women. They too spoke of love, trust and commitment in their relationships. They too had worked out conflicts over money and religion. But many of them also complained about lack of communication. "It's one-sided," said one woman. "All the communication is going from me to him." Another woman wrote that her marriage was "perfect from the outside, lonely from the inside," because of a lack of communication. The teacher in St. Louis told us that she and her husband were considered a model couple by others, but she too admitted, "I suffer from too little sharing."

Few women analyzed their marriages as closely as Eleanor did. We often received one-word replies to the question "How do you rate your marriage now?"—especially from older women. Answers such as "great," "the best," and "excellent" didn't really tell us very much. Younger women and unhappier women tended to go into more detail. One exception was Phyllis, the professor's wife, who rated her marriage "very strong" and told us why:

As the child of divorced parents, a good marriage was for me a high priority, probably the priority. Before my children my marriage comes first and I think that the children know this.

I am not as comfortable with anyone else as I am with Jim. I don't love anyone else as much as I do Jim, and I wouldn't make the sacrifices I've made for anyone but Jim. He feels the same about me. Jim and I can talk about everything.

Audrey, the psychologist, who is married to an attorney, explained that the secret of her happy marriage was communication:

When we have good times, and by good time I mean evenings when my husband can be home for dinner and we have an hour when we can talk, then the marriage is completely happy. The only time we seem to have conflicts is when we're out of communication.

We can go on for a while, and then one or the other feels out of whack, and we call a halt and say "time to go out for dinner, alone, no kids"—that has really paid off. Now our relationship has reached a stage where we can go two or three weeks and not be in communication because we know that as soon as one of us feels the need, we can reconnect.

One of the most troubled answers to the question "How do you rate your marriage now?" came from a young government official's wife named Joanne, who lives in Washington, D.C.:

My husband told me at Thanksgiving when I complained about his distant behavior, "My success has gone to my head. I'm so much smarter than I ever thought I was. My position means everything. My family is not a priority."

This marriage has since ended in divorce. A military wife in San Diego, who rated her marriage "fairly good, with peaks and valleys" on page one of the questionnaire, typed this note at the end:

During the time I received and was filling out this question-naire, my husband has left the household, stating that he can't take the pressures I put on him. This is a man who has been making it home approximately five days per month for the last four months . . . and [he] says I put too much pressure on him. Funny, huh?

Many women who felt they had good marriages admitted that they had gone through difficult periods with their husbands. They all maintained that their marriages were stronger for having been tested.

The Job

A wife's attitude toward her husband's work is only one of the many factors that determine a successful marriage, but it is an important factor. Does she love his career as one of the most powerful Senators in America? Does she hate his career as a spy? Does she find banking and bankers dull? Is she proud of his military manner? We asked wives at the top to tell us how they felt about "the job."

Many had mixed feelings. Maria, the diplomat's wife, said that this was certainly true of her:

> *I have a love/hate feeling for his work. I hate the hours, hate the pressure, the stress on him, the family and me. The love part is that I feel he's doing something that means something.*
>
> *If he were working fourteen hours a day selling Colgate toothpaste, forget it. We would never have lasted this long. I back him because I feel what he does makes a difference in this world. You can sweep a lot of ill feelings and frustrations into this box.*
>
> *Obviously sometimes I wish he would sell toothpaste so I could at least complain. This way there's guilt. He wraps himself in the American flag, and my problems can't compete with the possible destruction of the United States. But I do believe in what he's doing, and half the time I'm wrapped in that flag with him.*

Joanne, the government official's wife, complained that her husband's job really affected his personality:

> *At work he is the chairman, and everybody looks up to him. Nobody dares be totally honest with him because their jobs depend on his approval of them. He works in an environment where he isn't challenged, let alone disagreed with. He's always the boss.*
>
> *My feeling is that after a while he couldn't come home anymore and take off that hat and stop being Mr. Chairman. I wanted him to be good old Pete, the man I married fifteen years ago. I think he resents me now for not treating him as something special, because that's the way everybody else treats him.*

Many wives felt that it was their role to keep him "good old Pete," pricking the balloon of his success and status at work. Sometimes this was good for the marriage, and the husband appreciated his wife's attitude. Sometimes he resented it.

Many women clearly took a great deal of pride in their husbands' success and in the kind of work they did. Peatsy Hollings, the wife of the junior Senator from South Carolina (and herself a former Senate staffer), felt that public service was a high calling. The wife of an executive in one of America's largest automobile companies felt the same about business:

> *It's an essential and important part of any democracy. Our basic freedom doesn't survive where business doesn't thrive. Having come from a family of lawyers and teachers, the corporate life was different for me.*
>
> *I am impressed with the ethics and breadth of America's larger corporations. From President Roosevelt, who governed when I was growing up, I might have expected otherwise.*

Several other wives told us that they were very enthusiastic about their husbands' jobs. Sandra, a journalist's wife and herself a writer for a larger city paper, wrote:

> *I'm still starry-eyed about journalism. I feel it contains the best and the brightest, a tough-minded bunch of skeptical realists.*

Maria said that if she were to have a career, it would be in the Foreign Service, like her husband's. She admitted that she had taken and passed the exam and then had decided that she didn't want to work full time while her children were growing up. She went on to say:

> *Believe it or not, sometimes when Tony comes home at ten at night, we talk about foreign affairs. His job has always been demanding, but he has made me feel like an important part of it.*

These couples often act as a team, and the husband's job becomes a large and positive part of the wife's identity. For many women, like Barbara Bush, wife of the Vice-President, this works very well. She told us:

> *I really enjoy the job. I like feeling I can help George, and I love the fascinating people we meet from all walks of life.*

There is no doubt that if a wife is naturally interested in what her husband does, it's a tremendous plus for the marriage, especially if he can share his work life with her.

We found that there were other women who didn't particularly relate to their husbands' jobs but enjoyed the benefits of these jobs. In the words of one woman:

> *I feel lucky he is in international business. The people we meet and the places we see are more than I ever imagined in my life.*
>
> *His job also provides me with more material benefits than I ever dreamed possible.*

Bonnie-Jean, the petite gray-haired wife of an economist, feels this way:

> *I'm not interested in economics except in what I need to read in the newspaper. My own interests lie elsewhere. But his job brings me into contact with many fascinating opportunities, and I enjoy them. It also brings pressures and problems.*

But the wife of a computer executive in California felt apprehensive about her husband's work:

> *I don't understand a lot of it. In fact, when he tells me what he is doing, sometimes I feel uneasy. I don't know how I would handle the job, and I guess I worry that he won't know what to do and that he will fail. This has never happened. He seems to be very good at what he does, but I still worry.*

Some of the most negative responses to the question "How do you feel about your husband's profession?" came from the wives of doctors and military men. These professions were seen as the most pressured, and were felt to be especially hard on wives. The wife of the head of a large clinic wrote:

> *It's a real rip-off. I'm disgusted with medicine and what it has become. When I was young, it was a humanitarian pursuit. Now it's big business.*

A surgeon's wife felt this way:

It's too all consuming. Workaholism is assumed to be a prerequisite. No one has a chance to rest on his laurels.

And an admiral's wife complained bitterly:

I detest his profession. The position of senior officers' wives is medieval, and there is never any escape from it. I also hate what it's done to him, closed him off to personal needs. It's made him a stranger to me. He seems to have lost touch with his own feelings.

The Navy takes all of his time, energy, and inflicts separation on us. And when push comes to shove, it's always the Navy, first, last and always.

He Never (Always, Sometimes) Listens

Thirty-six percent of the women questioned said that their husbands were definitely interested in their concerns, 11 percent said their husbands were getting better about it, 14 percent said "no" and 39 percent said "yes, but . . ." When the man's job takes precedence over all else, it often erodes communication between husband and wife, and in time this breeds resentment. Many women mentioned this. Resentment develops because wives feel overburdened by everyday problems which they are forced to handle alone. If a husband isn't responsive to his wife's feelings, the resentment grows. It is not surprising that women who felt their husbands had little interest in their concerns also rated their marriages as poor. A divorcee wrote:

This was the problem. He not only was not interested in my concerns, he, while never directly undermining them, always made it hard for me to do anything away from home. Things I did at home were fine. He built me a darkroom and a studio for painting but raised hell when I wanted to take classes away from home.

Another woman complained:

He used to try to be [interested in what I was doing]; now he can't be bothered, and I really resent that because I am an intelligent, talented, multifaceted woman.

She described her marriage as "very uneven, with the lows more depressive than ever and the highs lacking romance, passion or joy."

A minister's wife wrote that her husband was generally uninterested in her and her pursuits, though he said he was. She has to "blow up periodically" to get his attention. She also had this to say:

> The longer we are married, the less I see of him, the less I am considered and the less time we have together. He takes me for granted. I must fight for time to communicate. When I raise hell and attribute any problem to the stress of his job, he turns a deaf ear. He really doesn't want to hear that at all.

And Joanne, whose marriage has since fallen apart, told us:

> He was mainly interested in maintaining a placid environment at home so he could concentrate on his work. He was always under a great deal of pressure, so I tended to let him ignore me because I knew he was busy, and I knew he was a very important person. But he left me anyway.

In a few cases, however, women felt that their husbands' lack of interest had forced them to grow and become more independent. Dottie Blackmun, wife of Supreme Court Judge Harry Blackmun, said:

> His work load is overwhelming, and the decisions are far-reaching. Most of the time he is engrossed with his own thoughts. I have long since learned to solve my own problems.

She rated her marriage as strong and takes pride in her own development.

In the "yes, but . . . " category, the "but" usually meant either "sometimes" or "in some things." Many wives said that their husbands were interested in anything having to do with house and family, but much less so in their wives' jobs or outside activities. "He wants me to be happy but is not interested in the details" was the general feeling. Others maintained that lack of time together was the problem and that the intense demands of their husbands' jobs left very little of him for them.

Still others spoke of degrees of interest. "Mildly interested and sympathetic," wrote Shirley. "Greatly concerned but on a theoretical level," said Jane, a China scholar married to a lawyer. "He's concerned if I'm depressed about a messy house, but he won't go so far as to help clean it up."

Louise said that her politician husband didn't want to hear about problems, especially if they involved the family:

> *A lot of my concerns are things he has put the quietus on, that I cannot even bring up with him. I'm frightened about it. There is one particular problem right now. I think our son needs to go to therapy, but I cannot bring this up with Warren. I'm losing sleep over it.*
>
> *Mike (our son) had school phobia, and I didn't know what it was. I just had this vomiting child. The pediatrician told us what it was and referred us to a psychiatrist. Mike really does need to divest himself of his anger and the hurt and resentment he feels about his father, and I know that can be done in a therapeutic situation. But Warren won't let him go. No parent likes to admit that their kid is in therapy because of what they've done.*

Women who told us that their husbands were interested in their concerns often mentioned that this hadn't always been the case. The wife of an Army major said that this was true of her husband:

> *Yes, [he's] very much [interested] now. But this only came about after years of holding feelings in, being the "good, patient and understanding wife." Now we talk about everything freely and honestly.*

A Senator's wife put it this way:

> *His interest is real, but his busy schedule does not permit him the time to contemplate my needs as I have traditionally ministered to his. However, I have learned to voice my concerns, and he has learned to understand them. But this came after many years of his not being interested or perhaps my believing that he wasn't interested. Of course, the more I share my own life with him, the more interested in them he becomes.*
>
> *By the way, it works the other way around too. When he really*

shares his feelings about his job with me, I find that I'm more interested in his *concerns.*

Why Am I Alone on Another Three-Day Weekend?

We asked our respondents if their husbands were often away from home. This question covered business trips as well as long working days and weekends spent at the office. The majority (93 percent) said "yes!" When asked how they felt about this, 50 percent said "resigned," 30 percent said "unhappy," and the remaining 20 percent admitted that they enjoyed having this time to themselves. "And it keeps us from always bugging each other," added the wife of one of America's busiest men.

The length and state of the marriage often affected wives' attitudes toward their husbands' absences. Those who rated their marriages as stable and happy seemed to be able to handle separations better than those who were less happily married, we were interested to discover.

Younger wives, especially those with small children, found absentee husbands the most irritating. They resented having to carry the responsibility for the household single-handedly. The wife of a Pittsburgh businessman complained:

He works ten to twelve hours a day, plus three or four trips a month. I feel he doesn't do his share in rearing the children, and he certainly avoids all the nuisances of running the household.

Another woman stated:

Yes, he's away a lot. I resent it. I'm glad he's working at what he likes to do and I'm glad we can buy nice things with the money he makes, but I wish he'd spend more time with me and the children. He could at least act like he'd rather be with us than at work. I know he's in the position to spend more time at home if he really wanted to.

Anger and frustration over their husbands' long hours built up in many young wives, and they reacted in negative ways. A writer, the wife of a Chicago stock broker, admitted that she took childish delight in getting back at her husband for coming home late. Harriet would eat dinner with the children and clean up, and when her husband, Steve, arrived home at 9:00 P.M., he would have to fend for himself. Another young mother was so resentful of her husband because of his long work hours that she boycotted all social functions at his company. "I was angry that they took him away so much of the time," she declared.

While their husbands are out of reach, these women have to cope with all sorts of problems and have to cope with them alone. The wife of a radio broadcaster told us:

> *I hate his being gone when important things are happening with the children, or when the car dies, or when the IRS is asking questions about our tax returns.*

And Sarah said of her spy husband:

> *While he's overseas bugging toilets in foreign embassies, I'm home unclogging our own.*

A young Congressman's wife wrote:

> *He's gone two weekends a month and ten days every six weeks. I have to be mother and father both. Besides, many of the things he does when he is away in the state are silly.*

Some women felt that their marriages were seriously threatened by the absences required by their husbands' jobs. The wife of a presidential staff assistant looked back gloomily on a time when she and her husband were forced to be apart:

> *We average five days a month* together. *He is away about two hundred days a year. The rest of the time he is tied up at work here. It's getting harder and harder to accept. He's kept up this pace for the last two and one half years and it's lonesome, all the disadvantages of being single and none of the advantages.*
>
> *I want to start a family and find it impossible. His absences and the pressures of his job affect my fertility, or lack of it. I'm also very nervous when I'm alone for extended periods of time.*

The wife of a Navy captain conducts her marriage almost exclusively by correspondence and doesn't like it that way:

He spends every week night away from home. Of the twenty-eight years we have been married we have spent twelve years apart due to sea duty. I had to be both mother and father to the children, and I hate it, despise it, loathe it.

Doctors' wives complained not only about their husbands' long hours at the office but also about the fact that they had to go back to work for emergencies. It was very hard to plan around this sort of schedule, they said.

Karen, the wife of the State Department employee, had another problem. She told us that the phone in their bedroom rang all night long and that she and her husband spent many nights in bed with Graham talking to the Secretary of State on the phone between them. "The bed wasn't built for three," she wrote, "and he calls at the most inopportune times."

Another complaint which surfaced had to do with husbands who were home but not really there. A salesman's wife from San Francisco told us that this was a problem in her marriage:

When he is at home, he is usually reading work-related materials and is only half there. I feel he spends too much time overpreparing for his work, but he feels driven to do so because he doesn't want anyone to know more about any subject than he does.

Eleanor, the banker's wife, wrote from Des Moines:

He works long days, but he always has some project going in the basement or garage which takes his spare time. I would like for him to be willing to spend that "spare time" with me doing things that we could enjoy together.

A car dealer's wife echoed these sentiments:

When he finally didn't have to work on Saturdays, I thought how lovely it would be, for the first time, to have family time together. But he had other ideas. He went out and enrolled in an art course.

Even though I felt that he deserved to spend his leisure time in a way meaningful and enjoyable for him, I also resented the fact that the class was from twelve to three on Saturdays, effectively eliminating any possibility of family activity. Then it occurred to me that he felt threatened by not having a work schedule to hide behind.

But as we stated above, half the women we questioned felt that they had adjusted to their husbands' inevitable absences, and many others said they had come to enjoy the time they had to themselves. These women also seemed to have happy marriages. How was this possible?

Some said that it was actually a way of life which had hidden benefits. Bonnie-Jean, the economist's wife, told us:

He travels several times a month and is often in town for conferences and dinners, with and without me. It was difficult when the children were small. Now it's just an accepted fact of life, and it makes us consider the quiet time together alone as something special and precious.

And Angela, happily married and the mother of grown children, said that now she isn't as resentful about having her husband away as she used to be. One "glorious week" on her own she read ten books. "It gives me time to catch up on things," she said, "and I think the separations help us to appreciate each other more." Some women had become so used to their husbands' traveling that they found it hard to imagine life any other way.

He used to travel about 75 percent of the time. His return changed our routine, so we were continually adjusting to his being gone and then to his being back. Now I don't think I could stand it if he were home every night!

said a manufacturer's wife from Toledo. A pilot's wife has learned to make the best of it:

He always brings [back] some kind of presents, and it's an opportunity to do more with the children, like go to McDonald's or a movie because we don't have to be home every night to greet him.

Several women told us that their husbands' attitudes toward their absences made a big difference. "Since I know he can't help it, and that he wants to be home as much as we want him home, I don't complain," said Pat Haig, the wife of the former Secretary of State. "Why make him feel guilty when he can't do anything about it?" And Audrey told us that just knowing that her lawyer husband would always take her phone calls, no matter how busy he was, helped a lot. "I don't call him over every little thing, but I know I could and that he would try to help with any problems I might have no matter what was going on at work. That makes all the difference," she said.

Time Together

A frequent comment made by the women we surveyed was that they had very little time alone with their husbands. With the men working ten to twelve hours per day (and sometimes more), the little time remaining had to be shared with children and other duties. The time together as a couple was often only "a few hours a month, if we're lucky" or "in an average week fifteen to thirty minutes to ourselves, and two weeks vacation a year." A doctor's wife said that she stayed up late to have a few minutes with her husband if he was home by midnight.

Peggy, the athletic mother of four and the wife of a governor who has spent many years in public office, told us that finding time together was an ongoing problem for her and her husband:

> We have a couple of nights a week to ourselves. This job is a killing one, and he works all the time. Weekends are the worst time as far as I'm concerned because he's there, but he's working at home. I really don't count on him for weekends, so if he's available to do something, I'm always surprised.
>
> He and I don't do any sports together. He is doing all the correspondence, all the letters, all the bills. He gets tons of letters. I feed him and give him a squeeze, and that's about it.
>
> I'm not really frustrated by anything he does, but I am sometimes frustrated by the way things have turned out.

The wife of an international businessman occasionally questions her way of life but feels that she has come to terms with it:

We really have lived separate lives, his with work, mine with kids, together for business and social affairs. Even now I take them to E.T., *and Adam goes to* A Midsummer Night's Sex Comedy.

I don't know if this is right or not, but it's all I've known. Sometimes I think I'm lucky, sometimes I think I've missed a lot, but I honestly don't know. It's the way for me, and I accept it.

Being together in a crowd at business or social gatherings does not make up for the lack of time alone. Jane, who is married to a prominent West Coast attorney, told us:

No, we don't have much time alone together, and this is a real problem. Even when we go out to dinner or a cocktail party, the expectation is that we talk to other people. At dinner husband and wife are often seated apart, and this bothers me sometimes. When one has five children and heavy church and school involvements, people are always chipping away at your time.

You need a chance to recharge your original relationship with your husband, which is the nucleus and raison d'être *of the family. You must be aggressive about saying no even to children, and extremely selective about invitations you accept.*

For some couples, though, being together in a crowd is not a problem. Sandra enjoys her husband's company in all circumstances:

We go out so often for business that we rarely want to go out just as a couple. We prefer to stay home together.

I don't think that "couple time" with my husband is any different from time with children or other people. I just like being with him, period. I love seeing him in his professional capacity, and we have a marvelous time just by ourselves too.

But being at the top often means rarely being alone together. Angela, the wife of the CEO of a Fortune 500 company, told us that she and her husband were seldom alone, even when they traveled together. "We're always in the company of the staff, crew, his driver and his associates," she complained. "Sometimes I wish we led a simpler life."

Several women complained that even when they were alone with their husbands, they were involved in separate activities. A consultant's wife said:

> We average a few working hours per week, including the grouchy morning ride to town if he's home and going to the local office. But much of this time together is two people singly doing separate chores, not quite the communicative sharing I had originally hoped for.

But the wife of a Midwest college president said:

> I have enough time with him, because he never relaxes. I don't like him around when I'm working, and when I'm not working, I'm relaxing, and since he doesn't know the meaning of the word, I don't really want him around then either.

Lack of communication was the most frequent complaint after lack of time together among the women we surveyed. A typical remark was:

> While my husband is with me in body, he's most often preoccupied with business matters. We have never had much communication. He can't discuss feelings, and it's hard to really talk to him about anything but technical matters.

The physical and intellectual demands that the jobs of successful men make on them often leave them completely drained after the workday. The wife of a New York executive said that her husband is almost catatonic by evening:

> He is such a tense and highly strung man. When he comes home, he makes himself a drink and sits down and doesn't speak for forty-five minutes. He needs to get his equilibrium again and unwind. Then he can talk.

Some women look forward to their husbands' return after a trip or a long day of work only to be disappointed at the way things turn out. Even though she has her hands full mothering five children and studying Chinese, Jane said she looked forward to time with her husband in the evening, but usually it did not turn out as she had planned.

Sometimes there will be several weeks when I hardly see him. He physically comes back to the house, but we don't have dinner together. I usually eat with the kids. I'm sorry to admit it, but I do.

And the other thing is, the nights I wait for him, I'm hungry and sometimes it's not such a good idea. He comes home tired and he'll go upstairs and change his clothes. I'll sit down with great expectations of having a really good time, but he's too tired.

Many women are respectful of the demands made on their husbands' time and voice no complaints. Phyllis, the professor's wife, declared:

In spite of the fact that we are often together much of the time, with the exception of one half-hour for dinner he is always working and I never interrupt his line of thought unless it's imperative.

For some unhappy wives, even a little time with their husbands is too much. Harriet, the stockbroker's wife, had this to say:

Since there's no harmony in our home, the time spent together is too much. We're totally incompatible and spend our time bickering. We never talk about anything personal anyway.

And Mildred, a seventy-five-year-old woman who was married for fifty-one years to an Orlando businessman, said that she didn't mind having very little time with her husband because:

He tended to belittle me every time he opened his mouth. He wasn't pleasant to be with at all. I try to understand his stresses, but he doesn't open up to anyone.

Although many of the women we talked to did regret not having more time alone with their husbands, the husbands often appeared satisfied with the amount of time they spent with their wives. A newscaster's wife said:

We have about twelve hours per week [together]. I'm a day person and he's a night person. We try to attend church together but it's sporadic. This is apparently enough for him.

The wife of a computer company president made a similar observation:

It seems to be enough time for him. He is not a homebody or a fixer but a goer, always on the go, full speed ahead.

What can couples do about the demands on their time? Some cut out or cut down on unnecessary socializing. Others try to spend at least one or two weekends a year alone, together. Getting the husband out of the house seems for many women a good way to get his attention. "We take evening walks or bike rides," said one woman. Another mentioned "talking walks together after dinner." A third goes horseback riding with her husband every weekend. When children are grown, there is much more time to be together as a couple. The wife of an advertising man told us:

Our children are raised and gone, so we frequently stay in town after work and attend theaters and concerts. And we're always together on weekends.

Dottie Blackmun accompanies her husband when he travels:

During Court recesses he gives law school graduation addresses, judges moot court competitions and speaks at judicial conferences. I always go with him and listen to all his speeches, attend all his seminars, all social events, everything. I'm interested in the subject and love making new friends.

Husband and wife can make the most of the little time they have together and find closeness even in doing the household chores that involve them both. One's attitude makes a tremendous difference, said Sandra. She admitted that she and her journalist husband "need to learn to play more together," but she told us that she appreciated being close to him even when they were not playing:

Over the last couple of weeks we had to wrestle with a broken hot-water heater. There was never enough hot water when you wanted it. We had to go down to the basement at two in the morning to relight the heater and would laugh about this. I was talking to my husband in a particularly close moment a couple of days ago and said that our being down in the basement together worrying about the hot-water heater was not a very romantic time, but it was a very close time, oddly enough.

A sense of humor and an eye for the ridiculous certainly help in times of broken hot-water heaters and broken vacation plans, but in the words of an internist's wife:

If you love someone, there's never enough time together.

What I Love Most About Him

When we asked our participants what they loved most about their husbands, we were conscious of encouraging them to look at their husbands' positive qualities, to think about them as separate from their success. The answers often overlapped with answers to the question, "Why did you marry your husband?" Happily married women said that they loved "his ability," "his brilliance and humility," "his goodness and integrity, his unselfishness, his concern for me and his children," "his strength and intellect." Maria said that her husband was a "complete person" and added:

He's an honorable and concerned man with the highest ideals, principles and integrity. He is also fascinating, sexy and fun.

Several women said simply "his body." Many others emphasized their husbands' sense of humor. Some went into greater detail. Bonnie-Jean, the economist's wife, mentioned her husband's "patience, patience, patience," and went on to say:

He is genuinely concerned and understanding of the needs of the various members of his family, from an aging father to a daughter with medical problems. He is a good listener and quick to point out a good plan for pursuing a given problem.

Many women looked to their husbands for leadership and got it. Many were also appreciated for their own contribution to their husbands' success. In the words of a professional athlete's wife:

He loves me and needs my approval and presence. He is always saying he would never be where he is without me.

Some women loved their husbands' vitality and unpredictability. "He's even-tempered, and he's never dull!" said Musha Brzezinski, who is married to the former head of the National Security Council.

What I Don't

On the other hand, lack of appreciation of their efforts to further their husbands' careers was one of the factors most often cited in answers to the negative part of this statement. A Senator's wife told us how frustrated she felt about this:

> *I act as his hostess, housekeeper and au pair. I don't think he's ever appreciated how much I contribute to his professional success. If I didn't function successfully in my role, he couldn't function as well, if at all, in his.*
>
> *I'm not asking for a medal. I just would like for him to acknowledge this once in a while, and I really get discouraged when he doesn't.*
>
> *Some of these women who take off and leave their husbands with the children do it just so their husbands will see that it's not that simple being married to a man who's married to his job. I would never do it, but it does seem ludicrous that he has a chauffeur and I have no help in the house.*

And Jennifer, who gave up her job as a lobbyist to marry her politician husband, said that she got the angriest when he:

> *refused to acknowledge my contributions to his success by looking good and being charming at public functions, helping him to make contacts and smoothing feathers that he may have ruffled by his sometimes abrupt manner.*

Other women became frustrated when their husbands gave their best efforts, time and enthusiasm to "the job." They felt left out and on the short end of his priorities. Often too these men took on heavy civic obligations. A car dealer's wife wrote:

He spends so much of his physical and mental energies on his business and raising funds for charities that there honestly isn't enough time left over for health, hobbies and home.

Mildred complained that her husband got so carried away with outside projects and local politics that he was overstrained and short-tempered and came home and "barked at the family." She was angry that by overdoing it he made unfair demands on those who loved him.

Many of the women we surveyed were furious when their husbands made them feel stupid. A colonel's wife said:

He treats me like I'm dumb. He doesn't agree with many of my statements or opinions, whether personal or on world affairs. He just says, "You're wrong," and it infuriates me.

Another wife said that her husband told her what were and what weren't acceptable topics for discussion at a business social function and belittled her opinions in front of the children.

Another frequent complaint was that husbands were uncommunicative and non-nurturing, that they lectured and dominated conversations without sharing their own feelings with their families. The wife of a doctor said that her husband "hears but doesn't listen; looks but doesn't see" and that he was unable to discuss anything personal.

But we also found several women who had difficulty completing the statement "I really get angry (or hurt, or frustrated) when my husband . . . " Peggy, the governor's wife, said:

I don't get angry at anything anymore. I've been through that. I used to get frustrated at waiting endlessly for him, though.

Her attitude was one of acceptance, and she rated her marriage as very good. And Audrey wrote:

I really don't allow it to build up. If I feel something is unfair, I say so at the time in a logical tone of voice.

She recommended this as a way of dealing with the frustrations and hurts of being married to a very successful man. She told us how she had worked out this approach:

I decided at one point that I would have to tell him that I was angry about having him come home in a foul mood, but that I had to do it at a moment when I wasn't angry, or it would just end up in a big battle. I did it, and it worked, and I've used the technique ever since.

I told him that if he's had a terrible day, I didn't expect him to come dancing in the door, but that he should just say, "I feel awful. I've had a terrible day, and if you have something bad to say to me, save it until tomorrow." He worked at it, and I haven't had to say anything like that for the last five years. Now he's gotten in the habit. I guess things like that become a habit. He really makes an effort to be pleasant, to talk to the kids, to see what's happened to them. I know it's an effort. The kids don't but I do.

While one woman felt frustrated that her husband "continually drops socks, towels, clothes on the floor," another woman couldn't find anything negative to say about her husband. She wrote:

I can't really answer this. Nothing he does upsets me. He even picks up his clothes!

The Good Effects of His Success

Most of the women we asked, with the exception of those whose marriages were very unhappy, could cite many benefits of their husbands' success, for their marriages and for their lives. Almost all spoke of freedom from financial worries, being able to afford a good education for their children and travel opportunities as the greatest benefits. One woman said simply:

I worry less about money, so I am more pleasant to be with.

Angela wrote:

It has given us all the material things any woman could want, like lovely homes, pool, tennis court, cars, clothes, jewels, etc. Also we have opportunities to travel first class all over the world, and security and prestige.

A doctor's wife was more equivocal:

> *The benefits of being married to a successful man are obviously the material security and the money. If other things are in line, this is great, but if the marriage isn't good, of course this means very little.*

Peggy told us:

> *I have met an unbelievable array of people, ranging from diplomats, presidents, Nobel prize winners and kings. Who wouldn't find that exciting?*

We found that another benefit that these women enjoyed was the status that their husbands' jobs gave them. They admitted that his "star dust" rubbed off on them too. Some also basked in public approval. One woman acknowledged that she was proud of the way others bowed and scraped before her husband but went on to say that it also helped her to recognize his humanity. "I'll never idolize any man since I know how human my husband is," she said.

Other women emphasized the fact that their husbands' success had given them opportunities to experience new things together, and they had therefore grown together. Bonnie-Jean wrote from New York:

> *It has broadened our life beyond belief. It has strengthened our marriage as we've worked together to advance his career. We have moved seven times, and this has solidified our family because with each move we have needed each other more and have shared the excitement of a new location and a new job. Everything he has done has enriched our lives tremendously. Each new "adventure" renews our marriage by a need to walk together in response to a new set of responsibilities.*

The wife of a Cabinet member put it this way:

> *His success has made him reflect on my contribution, not demanding that he be home but allowing him the freedom to "climb." It has created a special tie, two small-town bumpkins successful together in the rat race of Washington.*

By approaching change as an opportunity for growth these couples have developed strong marriages as the primary benefit of success.

Several women mentioned that their husbands' positions had been an assist in their own career development. It had opened doors to them that otherwise would have been closed. An artist said that her husband's position helped her market her art, and Charlotte, just out of law school, frankly admitted to using her husband's contacts to land her first job.

The wife of a governor told us that she thought that the wives of prominent men were very interesting to other men:

> *My husband's position has been a very good entree for me socially. Look at the fringe benefits. Even if this marriage is not going to work, isn't it more interesting to be the ex-wife of a governor than the ex-wife of anybody else?*

Another benefit of being married to successful men was increased self-confidence and self-esteem among their wives. Although the number of women who mentioned these qualities was far smaller than the number who cited financial benefits, their answers were very interesting. Again, these women seemed to be able to turn negative experiences into positive ones. Here are the words of an executive's wife from Philadelphia:

> *Because he has always been gone a lot, I have become very self-sufficient and confident. I had to do things alone and suc-ceeded. I learned how to take care of problems as they arose without support from him. I learned my own strength even though I didn't truly want to do many of these things on my own.*

And Bonnie-Jean told us:

> *It has forced me to grow. I was shy, insecure, dependent, in spite of high hopes going into this marriage. It was essential that I grow to meet the challenges of his career, and real growth is almost always painful. But looking back, it was the best thing that could have happened to me.*

The Bad Effects of His Success

Eighty-four percent of the women we questioned told us that lack of time together was the single worst effect of their husbands' success. He was never there, too busy, too preoccupied. Often this complaint was accompanied by the feeling that success had caused them to grow apart rather than closer. Some women differentiated between the years of struggling to succeed and those after success had been attained. One said, "I think his striving for success cost us our closeness, although now that he *has* success, we are rediscovering it." Others mentioned that they had drifted apart "while he was climbing the ladder" and that they really didn't know their husbands very well anymore. "He's so different from the man I married," said Joanne. Shirley, a Washington wife, told us:

> *I feel he has moved beyond me. The people he works with and deals with during the day are far different from the people I work with.*
>
> *He works with policy makers, and I work with welfare recipients. My colleagues are other nurses, and his peers are managers and persons in high positions.*

When we interviewed her, she said:

> *Peter has grown way past me in sophistication. At a dinner at the White House I feel all thumbs and left feet, never knowing for sure that I'm saying or doing the right thing. He is totally comfortable. It's a deep-down feeling. I feel out of place, and he doesn't.*
>
> *The only time Peter's nervous there is when he has his family around the President or the Vice-President. He's afraid that we're going to embarrass him or upset things somehow.*
>
> *He likes the fast track, and I don't. I have to admit that it is exciting once in a while to do something like that, but it's not worth the cost. And it doesn't contribute to the things I really care about, it takes away from them.*

Other women said that success had changed their husbands, that they had become so used to dominating people at work that they fell into the same behavior at home. A doctor's wife complained that at times her husband's ego seemed "overly active," which made it more difficult to like him. Harriet went into more detail:

> *At the job Steve is placed on a pedestal by hundreds of people. He also has a small personal staff that caters to his needs. His only close friends are people who work for him, people who are not likely to want to displease him with honest appraisals of his behavior. He has no friends outside the business to give him a fresh perspective on himself. I have become an alien to him.*

And Betsy, the outspoken and buxom wife of a nationally known scientist, told us:

> *My husband, Otis, is constantly being pursued as the "authority" on everything. He dominates a party because people look to him to do so. They ply him with drink, and the lecture begins.*

Another bad effect of their husbands' success was the opposite of what some women cited as a good effect. While several mentioned that they had developed greater self-confidence and self-esteem through having to cope with the pressures of their husbands' success, others said just the opposite: Their husbands' success had undermined their own self-esteem. In the words of Eleanor:

> *Hank's success has reversed our personalities in a way. The more self-assured he has become, the less I've become. I have actually become more a part of him than an individual.*

The wife of a successful manufacturer blamed herself for living in the shadow of her husband's success for too long:

> *While he grew and continues to grow more self-confident and positive, I have grown "bitchy" and somewhat bitter because I did not do what I wanted to do for the past twenty years. I have constant conflicts about being able to make a career for myself when my youngest child leaves because I have not furthered my career for all this time.*

Another woman said simply, "I don't feel as important as he is."

Several wives complained that their husbands' jobs forced them into a certain role. Ministers' wives felt this particularly, and sometimes the more successful the husband became, the more burdensome the role of "minister's wife" was. Sarah, the CIA agent's wife, told us that her husband's job demanded that she be perfect, that she never do anything which would jeopardize his position. She also told us about the role that Bruce's job forced *him* to play:

> *The intelligence mentality is a very interesting thing. It's a matter of life imitating art, imitating life. For example, in the latest James Bond movie, he drinks pisco sours, so you found all the local bars around McLean [Virginia—where the CIA is located] having a run on pisco sours for the next couple of months. The trench coat, a certain kind of pipe—they all want to live up to this movie image of a spy. It's really comical. You're expected to drive a fast car and womanize. You can't have a secret agent with four kids and a station wagon.*

Finally a small percentage of the wives we surveyed blamed their husbands' success for the breakup of their marriages. Michelle, the unhappy ex-wife of a diplomat, told us that her husband had grown less and less interested in his family and the outside world as he rose higher and higher in the corps. When he landed one of the top career jobs, their marriage ended:

> *He was never home, or if he was, he was asleep. Then he would get up at five-thirty the next morning to beat the traffic to work. Even on Sundays he just waited for that call from the office asking him to come in to solve a crisis.*
>
> *The most disturbing part for me was that this was like a shot in the arm to him. Whenever they called him back in because of a crisis, it was like the addict getting his drug, his fix. It was the only thing that turned him on anymore.*

To Leave or Not to Leave

Our questionnaire ended the section on marriage with the questions "Have you ever considered leaving your husband?" and "If so, why didn't you?" We were interested in finding out just how happy or unhappy these women were being married to successful husbands and how committed they were to their marriages. We discovered that although two thirds admitted to having considered leaving at one time or another ("Really now, haven't we all?" said one), only 3 percent had actually walked out of their marriages for good. And only a few had gone as far as consulting a lawyer about it. One third of the wives surveyed replied "no" or "never" to the question.

Women between thirty-five and forty-five had considered leaving the most often. The reasons given for wanting to leave ranged from feeling trapped, the fear of stagnation and extramarital affairs—both the husband's and the wife's—to alcoholism and general incompatibility. Feeling unloved and unappreciated made some women contemplate divorce. The wife of the manager of a truck company told us:

> *I don't like feeling second to a pickup truck. It's hard to compete with his work when he loves it so much. But I went through one divorce and know how much it hurt my first husband when I left him.*
>
> *I wasn't willing to accept being second to my husband's job, so I went into therapy and discovered me! I didn't leave him because I love him.*

In a few cases husbands had become abusive of their wives and families. An insurance company president's wife said:

> *I have been made to feel unimportant and not a person. His anger can bring out a lot of fear in me. We argue a lot about the children and how to treat them.*
>
> *I stayed because I wasn't sure I would be better off if I left, and I was fearful of the chaos caused by a divorce and the upheaval of breaking up the family. I've kept hoping that things would work out and would change for the better.*

The wife of a Southern judge lamented:

> *Randolf abuses me and the children emotionally. Days can go by when we all dread his coming home. But I have stood up to him, forced the issue and made it clear that I would leave if the atmosphere did not improve.*

We found that many women had hung on to miserable marriages because they felt that they couldn't make it on their own. Financial dependence and lack of self-confidence had tied them to their husbands. A doctor's wife told us:

> *I cannot stand the way my husband treats me. His total disregard for my feelings has made me feel I'd be better off without him, but I haven't been able to get enough money together. I wish he'd die sometimes.*

Betsy, who had worked in the lab with her scientist husband when they were first married, gradually dropped her career to encourage him in his. As he became more and more prominent, his ego grew too, until she felt completely dominated by him and his success. She told us:

> *Our marriage has been a triumph of incompatibility, but I stay for purely selfish reasons. Would I be better off alone? Could I earn my own living? Could I live in the manner to which I am accustomed? The answers seem to be negative to all these questions.*
>
> *I am back in a dependent role since my work has fallen away to nothing and my scientific skills need reviving. I just don't have the money myself, and that's what it takes, because I know he wouldn't give me a penny. Money and preparation. One cannot just walk out cold at age fifty and survive.*

The majority of women who had considered leaving their husbands told us about particular events or problems in their lives which they felt unable to cope with. The problems were most often infidelity and alcoholism. A Navy wife admitted that she had considered leaving her husband because of his drinking:

> *He was an alcoholic. He was sent to alcoholic rehab (a real military tabu), and it literally changed our lives together. But now he has turned all that compulsive energy that he put into drinking into the pursuit of his job. He can't seem to communicate with me, and I feel cut off and very alone most of the time.*
>
> *I didn't leave him because I genuinely cared for him and really detested the idea of him becoming what I have seen so many single men become, lonely, cutoff, going to work, into a bar, and falling*

*into bed and doing the same thing the next day. Turning back into
an alcoholic.*

The wife of a school superintendent was understanding and compassionate when faced with the same problem in her marriage:

*He drank too much. When he was home, he would pick on me
and the children when he had had too much to drink.*

*I realized that alcoholism was an illness. We both went for
treatment and learned that we wanted to make it together. I still
love him very much.*

Infidelity on the part of husband or wife was also mentioned. In the following quote a congressman's wife tells how she reacted to this problem:

*It was fourteen years ago. He betrayed the trust of the marriage
and had an affair with another woman. I think it came from his
suddenly being such a big shot. But I felt it was a transitory thing
and that he really didn't want to leave.*

*Some very rough years ensued, but working out this situation
made our marriage infinitely stronger. That is the only time I ever
considered leaving him. I guess life is really so exciting with him,
why would I want to be a lonely, empty person just to prove he had
made a mistake for which he was very regretful?*

And Harriet told us about her own affair:

*Disillusionment, futility and loneliness made me turn to someone else. He gives me an awful lot of time and attention, unlike
my husband.*

*But I can't leave. I've grown very accustomed to this life-style
with all its advantages. My children have never known not being
able to buy what they wanted.*

Other women said that it was nothing as dramatic as infidelity or alcoholism that had made them consider leaving their husbands but rather a feeling of general dissatisfaction with themselves or their life-style. A New York executive's wife spoke of sometimes yearning for a quiet life in a beach cottage. But she added:

I realize that this is complete fantasy. I am realistic enough to know that the grass only seems *greener on the other side, and I love him.*

A Senator's wife confessed that at one period of her life she felt that she was unworthy of her husband's love:

I sometimes felt overshadowed by his brilliance and reputation. I'm well-educated, bright, personable and had a successful career myself, but I felt comparatively worthless. I failed to see the success in my parenting and wifing profession as comparable to his. I knew this was my problem, but he was part of it somehow.

Now I recognize that it's mainly up to me to build up my self-esteem more, so that I see him as just different, not incomparably better.

When we asked the women who had considered leaving why they hadn't, many mentioned religious reasons. "God's presence during our wedding," said one. "I made a holy vow to stay with him," replied another. This was a kind of safety catch for many marriages, keeping couples together through bad times. Children were another safety catch. One woman admitted to having been unhappy at one period but felt she really didn't have anywhere else to go with her eight children. 'I couldn't leave, I didn't leave, and I'm glad now,' she told us.

Summing Up

Marriage seems to be an institution that still works for most wives of successful men. A banker's wife summed it up this way:

Of course I have considered leaving him! Every marriage has such moments if people are really in touch with their feelings. Why? Because we couldn't childishly force each other to be what we thought we wanted and needed. Eventually we came to realize that we were lucky with what we had.

Not that we don't still play these games from time to time, but we are more skilled at recognizing sooner such self-defeating patterns.

Many women who rated their marriages high said that good communication between husband and wife was essential. These women were able to tell their husbands how they felt about some of the strains that success put on them. Their husbands were able to listen without feeling threatened or guilt ridden. The women with strong marriages also shared their outside activities with their husbands and involved them as much as possible in their own concerns. And their husbands took an interest in their pursuits even if these didn't directly involve them.

On the other hand, there was a strong consensus among the women we questioned that they would have liked their husbands to be *more* interested in them. Most realized that this was difficult because of the many demands on a successful man's time, but they felt it was more a question of attitude than hours. Their husbands' interest in their concerns made them feel important, the lack of it just the opposite.

Guidelines

1. Try not to resent the time you and your husband have to be apart. He probably feels as bad about it as you do.
2. Plan the time when you are on your own for self-development. Try to see it as a chance to develop independence within the security of marriage.
3. Plan carefully so there is enough time for you and your husband to be alone together.
4. If you find something is bothering you, tell him, don't let it build up. But choose a time when you feel relatively calm.
5. Don't forget why you married him in the first place. Reminding yourself of his good qualities from time to time helps keep the bad in proportion.

2

CHILDREN

Helen

Helen is the wife of one of New York's most influential businessmen. His picture and opinions appear often in the daily press. His power is enormous. Helen herself is a diminutive woman of sixty-six, one year younger than her husband. We interviewed her in her suburban home, which she had decorated herself in warm yellows and oranges. Devoted to her husband, whose inner tones are more somber, she told us that she was still learning how to handle him after thirty-eight years of marriage. She said that when he comes home from work, he can be one of two or three different people, depending on the kind of day he's had. Unfortunately, if he's in a bad mood, she still thinks it's her fault.

His workload is overwhelming, but he is able to handle it because he is very well organized. He pushes himself hard, but he pushes other people too and makes them feel guilty because of his superior efficiency. Helen feels that it is her husband's hard-driving personality and perfectionism that made growing up very difficult for their children, who are now in their thirties:

When you have this kind of man who drives himself so hard, he is very impatient with anyone who won't push themselves that hard. The children must feel it too. Our elder daughter had a very low sense of self-esteem. Our middle child didn't have quite as much of a struggle, probably because he was more like his father.

The oldest and youngest were super-intelligent, but they both had a terrible time getting started. They both made unfortunate first marriages. It was just heart-rending. As a matter of fact, my husband said he couldn't go to their weddings, but I just had to go.

One of them used to say to me, "Mother, it doesn't matter what you tell me, how great you think I am, I have to feel that way inside," which is true. But why did she feel this way?

I think it was just the way my husband was and what he expected. He expected a lot of them, but it wasn't that he told them they had to do this and that. One of them said, "Nobody ever says anything, but there's no doubt living in this family that we have to be achievers."

We never actually told them that they all had to get A's, but it was all there. At mealtimes he'd sit there, and instead of listening to them he was always picking on them. I'm sure it was because other things were bothering him and he had to take it out on someone, but I've always thought it so unfair to take things out on a person who hasn't done anything.

Looking back on her marriage and at her children, Helen says she would have done some things differently. She feels that the women's movement has helped women assert themselves more and says that a book called *Pulling Your Own Strings** by Dr. Wayne Dyer gave her a new perspective on herself. She now believes that an incident which happened many years ago could have turned out quite differently:

When our daughter was a teenager, she had an asthmatic condition. Once I had a medical appointment in another city for some special tests which I absolutely had to keep. That's the only time I've ever had to leave anybody in the lurch, and it's haunted me ever since.

I told my daughter that I would be home at a certain time and if she needed anything, to call her father at work. Well, she did have a crisis and called my husband, who had to leave work and come home.

---

*New York: Avon Books, 1979.

After that he made me feel in no uncertain terms that I had no right to ever leave home, so he wouldn't ever again have to come home because of a problem with one of the children.

Now I would have said, "Look, these are your children too, and once in a while I'm not going to be able to be here." If I had had the women's movement behind me, it would have helped.

If I had been firm, I could have achieved something, and it would have been better for the kids too. But I didn't say anything. I just seethed inside!

Seemingly unaware of his all-important influence on his children, Helen's husband often remarked that he didn't know why none of them had amounted to anything. He was disappointed in all three. But, she said, things had recently improved, and she could now acknowledge positive qualities that the children had learned from their father.

Our younger daughter has been a rebel. She sailed away seven years ago to the West Indies and has crewed professionally there and in the Mediterranean. She wanted to prove to herself that she could cut the umbilical cord and survive without us. Her growing self-esteem is based on her own virtues: honesty, integrity, dependability. Many of these qualities she got from her father.

Our older daughter is getting her doctorate in clinical psychology. She is almost thirty-six and has a couple of years to go. She is finally finding her identity in the pride she has in what she is accomplishing.

It has been interesting though often heartbreaking to watch this development. While both daughters have had trouble living up to their father's expectations, they have become stronger individuals as a consequence. Now that they are earning their father's approval, my daughters and my husband are able to enjoy each other at last.

Men at the Top as Role Models

The children of very successful men often have problems with self-esteem for several reasons. First, men at the top are role models who are hard to live up to. Children in the throes of growing up compare themselves with men who are at the height of their success. They imagine that their fathers were enormously successful as children too, though this is seldom the case.

Second, if they inherit their fathers' perfectionism and inner drive, life is difficult because they see themselves as failures even when they aren't. And if they don't inherit their fathers' perfectionism, they feel driven by it.

Often too these men are emotionally uncommunicative, leaving wife and children guessing as to the reasons behind anger and criticism. And their father's long hours make the children of a man at the top wonder about his priorities. Fortunately some successful men are able to balance the conflicting demands of work and family. However, the majority of the women surveyed expressed dissatisfaction with the relationship between father and children.

The wife of a university president put it this way:

We are seen as lazy if we can't maintain the same speed. My son works with his father, but I can really see why they say so many very successful men have sons who sit back and become basketweavers, because the joy of working just isn't there.

My husband doesn't really pay attention to their emotional needs. John has a picture of what he wants them to be in the future, and he expects them to function like little adults now. He demands an awful lot of them. When he comes home, he spends so much of his short time criticizing their failures, ordering them around, yelling at them. As much as he really wishes he had a good relationship with them, he has not had time to develop that relationship.

They do love him, which hurts even more because they want to please him, and they know they don't. Right now I could be separated from him and the children would develop just fine. I used to think that they had to have both parents, but sometimes that is not true. His role is predominately negative but with all the good intentions in the world.

He does loving, generous things from time to time, but he

forgets about their emotional needs. I gave him a book once called How to Father,* *and he read part of it and then stopped. He said that the book made him feel so bad he couldn't read anymore. It got him thinking, and thinking about his role as a father was painful for him.*

It was painful for John to think about his relationship with his children, so he spent more time at work. There he could feel that he was "doing it all for them" by providing them with material goods and "the best damn education money can buy." Ironically the qualities that propel a man to the top professionally, a strong inner drive and a certain necessary ruthlessness, are the very things that often make it difficult for him to be a good father. Perhaps there is also a degree of egotism necessary to get to the top that does not leave room for close family relationships.

Peggy, while acknowledging that her politician husband loved his children deeply, admitted that he was personally quite removed from them and their problems. He took them to lunch from time to time, "to prove that he was a good father," but both children and father found these occasions rather embarrassing. They just did not have that much to say to one another.

The Wife as Mediator

Lack of communication between father and children usually burdens the wife with the role of mediator. She tries to soften her husband's demands while at the same time helping the children to meet them. The wife of a famous physician told us that she often found herself in this position:

> *There are certain expectations that he has of his children that are never said outright but are very clear. He expects a great deal and has a very strong personality. Things are always black or white with him, never gray.*
> *He needs me to be the gray part of his life. That's the role I*

*Dr. Fitzhugh Dodson, New York: New American Library Signet, 1975.

play all the time. I play it intervening with the children, intervening with the staff problems he brings home to me. I have been a softener since the day I married the man.

Harriet put it more negatively:

When Steve does have time with the children, he only wants to do with them what he wants to do, things they don't care about, so unfortunately they don't enjoy being around him very much. It's a very superficial relationship. I don't think he's ever "talked" with them.

They feel distant, not comfortable at all talking to him about their thoughts.

Both of them come to me and ask that I approach their father on their behalf, but at my suggestion that they seek him out themselves, they often just skip it.

In any sticky situation Steve expects me to deal with the children, stating that he has enough problems to sort out himself. I only call him from the emergency room of the hospital.

However, we found that when wives refused to mediate between father and children, when they encouraged him to become involved with them on a daily basis, the whole family gained enormously. Carol, the wife of an extremely high-powered man, told us that they had reached a turning point in their family life about a year before. One night her husband had come home late, exhausted as usual. Her son needed help with his math. The father was impatient, the son got mad and stormed off to his room. Telling her husband that this time he had to follow up whether he was tired or not, Carol refused to intervene.

My husband went up to Brad's room, closed the door and listened to all the grievances of a screaming child. They were at it about a half-hour, with Brad crying and my husband calming him, when the office called. Eliot refused to take the call, saying he was busy and couldn't be interrupted.

With these magic words the boy quieted down. He finally felt that he was more important than the office, even when he was being difficult.

*They finished the math problems and emerged arm in arm.
Eliot ate his dinner even later than usual that night, but his
relationship with Brad improved and so did Brad's self-esteem.*

The desire to find a smiling wife and happy children waiting at
home is a very natural one for a man who has put in long hours at
work. Yet it is not always possible, nor necessarily desirable. Much
of the work of parenting is done under less than idyllic conditions,
and men who involve themselves constructively with whatever is
going on at home, be it good or bad, build more rewarding relationships with their families. Wives who encourage this are not being
selfish, they are helping their husbands to be good fathers.

Typically, when Eliot realized what his son needed from him, he
put as much effort into succeeding with his family as he did into his
job. Sensitive to failure on any front and used to demanding the best
from himself, he became an excellent father.

Maria told us that once her husband decided it was important to
spend time and energy on the children, he enjoyed it in a new way.
After a forced separation during an overseas tour Tony realized how
much he cared about his family:

*From then on he was pleased to be with them and would be sure
to make time for it, even leaving work early occasionally to see our
son play in athletic competitions or going to a play our daughter
was in three or four evenings (the whole run!). He now spends a
lot of time just talking with them. He feels it is hard to make up
for the time he avoided being with them, but he really wants to be
with them, for pleasure now as well as need.*

Lack of Time Together

Virtually all the women we surveyed said that the single biggest
problem with being married to men at the top was the lack of time
for the family. The wife of a congressman complained:

*His schedule in the House means we always do everything
around when he is available. He comes first in any family plans,
so we miss vacations, family gatherings, school activities, etc.*

This situation is not unique to Washington. From a cattle ranch in Wyoming a woman wrote:

> *The children and I have simply learned to do any and all things with the very real possibility that husband/father may or may not be present.*

And a young wife, the mother of a four-year-old, lamented:

> *Another Christmas, Easter, or Thanksgiving without Daddy seems particularly hard to explain to a young child.*

However, Musha Brzezinski told us that her forced role as an "only parent" was an advantage in a way. Because her husband was so often absent, she had to learn all sorts of masculine sports with her sons, as well as take them hunting and fishing. She didn't feel this was a burden at all but enjoyed it tremendously.

For most wives, however, it was very difficult to cope as "a single woman who just happens to be the mother of . . . children." Helping the children cope could be even trickier. Jane, the China scholar from Los Angeles, described the experience:

> *We have neighbors across the street, and he's a real nine-to-fiver, nine to four-thirty if possible. My daughter, Lucy, is their daughter's best friend. One day she came home in tears because her friend's father had come home from work and said, "You have to go home now, Lucy, because I'm going to play with Susan."*
>
> *I sat down on the front steps with Lucy, and she cried and cried, and I just let her. Then she said, "Mommy, you know, the real thing is that Daddy never comes home and plays with me," and I said, "I was waiting for you to say that, honey, I knew that was it." She also told me during that conversation that she feels like we're divorced. By the time her father gets home at night, either she's in bed or it's a few minutes before bedtime.*

Building Closeness When There's No Time

Knowing how important her father was to Lucy, Jane encouraged him to make a fuss over her when he was home. Now he sometimes takes Lucy out for "dates," no friends or other family members present. She chooses where they go, and he talks about what she wants to talk about. He is actually spending the kind of time with her that divorced fathers spend with their children, though he and his wife are still married. It has meant even less time with her husband for Jane, but she agreed that it was worth it.

Unfortunately it is impossible for a wife to truly comprehend just how much time her husband *must* spend away from his family. Professional success demands extraordinary effort, and the men who reach the top are the men who are willing and able to expend that effort. This is sometimes very hard for a wife to accept, even though she knows intellectually why he's doing it. Eleanor still remembers a painful experience in her early married years:

> *I was a very young wife with two babies, and it was Christmas Eve. I'll never forget it. It was about four o'clock in the afternoon. We lived in a modest neighborhood at the time with lots of close neighbors. Everybody else's Daddy was home. I had these two little kids.*
>
> *I remember that we had some lights that had to go up outside that he hadn't been able to do, and I remember that being one of the worst times of my marriage. Yet when I bring that up or mention it, his reaction is, "You will never forget that, will you?"*
>
> *He did come home that night, but the corporation for which he works closed long before that. He was the last one there because he was on his way up and that was that.*

Another woman said that she knew her husband felt that his family was very important but it was hard for him to convey this to his wife and children when he was under such extreme pressure at work. She continued:

> *There was a time when I felt that we were at the bottom of his list of his priorities, and he was very upset that we would think this way. He kept saying that it wasn't true.*
>
> *Then both of us had some counseling, and the point was brought out that if my feelings were that way, then there had to*

be something to it. Now that I know we come first, it's helped enormously.

Carol, married to a busy top executive, told us that marriage counseling had also helped her deal with her anger at Eliot's long absences. During the six months of counseling she really "heard" how much her husband loved his family and came to feel that he "was doing it all for them" even though it often looked like just the opposite.

Businessmen, lawyers, politicians and many other men at the top have work demands which simply do not allow for very much time at home. Carol reported that Eliot rose at 5:30 in the morning, making family breakfasts impossible, left the house at six and returned home between nine and 9:30 at night, which ruled out family dinners as well. He also worked most of Saturday and put in several hours at the office before church on Sunday. As much as he wanted to be home, he couldn't be. He traveled too and returned from his trips full of guilt and bearing gifts. Then he became Santa Claus to his three small children, leaving Carol to be the disciplinarian. He spent so little time with his children that he really hated to discipline them at all, so even his time at home presented problems for them.

Diplomats

In a category all by themselves, diplomats' wives have some extra burdens. Frequent international moves are very hard on the family. Heavy social demands take both mother and father away from the children. Maria's son asked his mother every morning if she was going out that night. He never complained, he just wanted to be prepared to handle it when the time came. Sometimes the wives of diplomats found the social life enjoyable, but in the words of one:

Sometimes I could just die. The last thing I want to do is wash my hair, get the glad rags on, cook the kids' dinner and race out the front door.

An overseas tour makes different demands, but the family faces them as a unit, not with the husband in one camp and the wife and children in another. The pace of life is slower; mercifully the rest of the world does not keep the long office hours that America does. Overseas tours can be a real godsend for exhausted, divided families. An example of how beneficial this time can be to an overstrained family was given by a young Foreign Service wife:

> *My husband was out of the country when our daughter, Julie, was born. As eager as he was to get his hands on her when he finally did come home, she would have nothing to do with him. He felt awful about this, but it didn't improve until we were transferred overseas when Julie was three.*
>
> *We went to a quiet country where the local people took life easy, and sometimes he even came home for lunch. It was heaven for all of us, and Julie finally realized that she had a father.*
>
> *One day she said to my husband that her name was Baby Tina and since she was a real baby, she couldn't walk or talk. He had to carry her around. My husband was delighted to get any kind of attention from her and went along with it, carrying "Baby Tina" around for the better part of a weekend. Then the game stopped of its own accord.*
>
> *Now, at the age of ten, Julie has no memory of this episode, but she does have a very close relationship with her father. She was able to fill in her missing babyhood with him.*

Ways of Coping

What can a father do when he has heavy work demands and no overseas tour to bail him out? It all depends on how much he is willing to do. If he cares about his children, he can communicate this caring in many different ways. He can tell his secretary to put their phone calls through no matter what. He can join in with whatever they are doing when he gets home and not expect to be treated as "Mr. Chairman" at home as well as at work. Fathers can also take time out for their children's athletics, school events and parent weekends.

One young White House staffer goes home at five every day to have dinner with his young children, helps tuck them in bed and then returns to his office for several more hours of work. Interestingly men who make a point of doing this kind of thing seem to gain rather than lose the respect of their colleagues.

Fathers can play the role of the "divorced" father without the trauma of a divorce, and possibly even prevent a divorce in the process. They can "court" their wife and children, making the little time they have together of real quality.

Most important of all, fathers can try to include their families in their work insofar as possible. A manufacturer's wife in the Midwest reported her husband's attempts to do this:

> *He tries to get them to understand what he does and why there was an emergency sometimes. He takes them to the cannery so that they can see the cans he had sold being used for peas and corn for instance.*

A Senator's wife told us that her husband took his children with him to the office on Saturdays and let them type on the electric typewriter and work the Xerox machine. His daughter told us that she thought her father's job must be pretty important because it took him away from them so much. She enjoyed being included in the "important" work too. The Senator also talked to his children about foreign affairs and introduced them to his staff. Then when the office called, his children took more interest in the conversation and didn't see the phone call as purely an interruption.

The greatest difficulty in including children at work is experienced by employees of the CIA and other top-secret government organizations. Not only are these men unable to take their children to see their place of work, but often they can't even tell their children where they work. If they can tell them, this causes other problems. Sarah told us that her son couldn't relate to what his father did because he had a negative concept of the CIA from the media.

But in most other cases there are many possibilities for developing closer relationships between fathers and their families. Usually a small effort produces great results. Unfortunately, however, if a man really doesn't consider his family important and isn't willing to work on his relationship with them, there is only so much his wife and children can do to improve things on their own. Sometimes a rift becomes deep enough, or the problems serious enough, to warrant professional counseling. If the whole family participates, this can be very effective in opening channels of communication and in reordering their priorities.

The effort to forge closer family relationships isn't the father's responsibility alone. Sandra, the mother of two, stressed this point in an interview. Children too can be encouraged to go out of their way to share their time with their father.

> *Mike has to give some also. When his father is home and working in the garden, then Mike had damn well better develop some interest in planting trees or something. If his father walks over to the store to pick up something, Mike can walk with him. I told him, "You can't expect your father to sit around while he is home just because you don't feel like walking or working or doing any of the things he does."*

Many men put in even longer working hours than necessary because they don't really feel part of the family unit. They are not comfortable at home. It takes an extra effort on the part of wife and children to make them feel important when they are together; it takes an extra effort on their part to make their families feel important when they are apart.

Serious Problems

A father's demanding schedule and nearly total immersion in his work can take a heavy toll on the emotional development of his children. Some of the problems that this causes are resolvable. Some aren't. In extreme instances these children are driven to suicide. This was true in the case of Alan, who killed himself in college. His politician father and his mother blame themselves for not taking the time to try to understand him when he was younger. The demands of campaigning and office holding left them too exhausted. And when a New York advertising executive started divorce proceedings after eighteen years of marriage so he could live with a twenty-four-year-old girl, his young son attempted suicide. Tanya, the boy's mother, acknowledged tearfully:

Both my children are in psychiatric care now. My thirteen-year-old daughter doesn't want to see [her father] anymore. She never knew him when we were married because he was always too busy at work, and now she can't forgive him for that and for leaving.

She craves affection and will do almost anything to get it. She is turned on by younger boys because she thinks she can get affection there. For the first two years after the separation she wouldn't come home. She would hang around the streets, refusing to come home. Did [her father] know that we were running around at eleven at night looking for her?

She's my responsibility now. Many times I feel she wants to blackmail me and threatens to pack her bag and leave. Now I've learned to react to it quite calmly. "Do you want to pack your bags? Go ahead and do it. Do you need money for the ride? Well, here it is."

The wife of an Alabama judge and the mother of a twenty-one-year-old was convinced that her husband's clear preference for his work had alienated her daughter.

Until her teens he never had enough time for her. And then he felt he didn't have anything in common with a teenage girl. He didn't like her language or her friends (with good reason). He just shrugs his shoulders.

Even today, while she is still at home, I am the bad guy. When she and I have problems, which is more often lately, he is convinced it is my fault. She had bad friends for most of her teens, and that affected schoolwork and resulted in some drugs. I honestly think that her rebellion is directed at him more than me. Maybe he'll pay attention to her if she misbehaves. At least negative attention is better than no attention at all.

Serious emotional problems could lie ahead as well for the son of the vice-president of a large multinational corporation. His mother wrote:

My husband and I have spent only the last weeks together in the last two years of marriage. I feel this is enough for me because now I enjoy my son. We share so many memories and good times without my husband.

At first I felt extremely lonely. But now my nine-year-old son and I have learned to depend on each other in time of stress. My son has learned to respect and admire women.

When a man's work demands so much time away from home, the wife has to decide for herself what her priorities are. The woman quoted above opted to ally herself with her son, staying at home with him while her husband traveled. Another wife we interviewed chose to travel with her husband, leaving her child at home. Unfortunately this caused emotional problems.

We were married for eighteen years before I had [my son]. I was forty-two and my husband fifty-six. I had worked for many years with my husband and accompanied him on all his business trips around the world. We led a very busy life, and when our son was born, I wasn't about to give this life up, neglect my husband and stay home. He would grow up soon enough and not need me anymore, but my husband still needed me.

We made sure that our son was always in excellent hands and hired nannies and nurses for him. He was a bright child but always a little withdrawn.

When he was nine years old, his schoolteacher suggested that we should have him tested for emotional problems. The tests cost nine hundred dollars. The psychiatrist who did the testing said that he had never seen such an unhappy child before.

We couldn't understand it. We gave him everything. Gradually we found out that one of his nannies who lived with us for several years forgot to give him his midnight snack when he was little. Our son felt nobody cared for him and nobody loved him, and [he] wanted to die. He thought we went away so often because we didn't want to be with him.

But we got him a good therapist. It cost us ten thousand dollars more, but he's fine now.

Special Privileges

The lives of the children of men at the top are full of privileges as well as problems. Money, and often a great deal of it, is one of the benefits they enjoy. With the money come private schools, expensive vacations and a luxurious life-style. These children meet interesting people and are often exposed to an intellectual atmosphere at home which gives them a learning advantage over their peers. Not surprisingly the children of politicians often turn their father's status to their advantage. William Mondale, in an interview with *The Washingtonian,* * said that when his father was Vice-President, it helped him get the "best girl." An ambassador's daughter told us that she enjoyed living in the official residence with a swimming pool and tennis courts, though it set her apart from her classmates, who said that the teacher would never dare give her bad grades because she was the daughter of the ambassador.

On the other hand, prominence can be painful too. The wife of an international financier reported that her children had turned on the evening news one night only to see their father being hung in effigy in a Mideast country. The experience had left permanent psychological scars, she said. A general's wife told us that her son had to suffer through a history class while the professor criticized his father's conduct in Vietnam.

Security worries the children of men at the top. The very wealthy often "go underground" for fear of kidnaping, according to Angela, the wife of one of America's richest men. Others, especially the children of politicians, fear for their fathers' lives. When Congressman Dellums of California was elected for the first term, his seven-year-old son was very upset. "Don't do that, Daddy," Brandy told him. "You'll be shot like Dr. King, and then we'll be all alone."

Children of public officials share their father's fish-bowl existence. "Being a public servant makes the family and all its activities public," one woman told us. When your father's on top, you're on top; when he's out, you're out.

*April 1982.

Peggy, the wife of a governor, said that her children naturally enjoy the perks but resent the problems that come with becoming "public property."

> *This is a very common thing in the children of prominent people. Our daughter went through a time of minding it very much. She was expected to be a certain way, or people would expect her to take the same stand on issues that her father did when she might not feel the same way or just didn't care about it at all.*
>
> *Why should anybody come up and accost her in the first place?*
>
> *When my husband ran for governor, she didn't want any part of it, but he talked to her and said how much he needed her help and support. She said, "Do you think I can get out of it?" and I answered, "I think your father will be hurt." She thought it over and decided she would do it, so she did and she did it beautifully.*
>
> *Once she got into it, she didn't mind as much, but she was still minding forcing herself into the mold of his daughter. This was what she minded, not giving the speeches and all the rest.*
>
> *There is prominence that is very personal. Everybody feels they know everything about you and want to know and have a right to know. You have to just tell the kids that this is unfortunately a normal thing and not to be bruised by it.*
>
> *My main concern when [my husband] was elected was that they would become big-headed. It's a very ego-raising experience.*
>
> *I told them that they were no more nor less than they were last year. "It's your father that has won this election, and we all come along as part of it, and we've all helped in some way." They still have troubles, not bad ones but ones you wish were not there.*

In His Footsteps

We asked the women we surveyed whether their sons wanted to follow in their father's footsteps, and whether they would want their daughters to marry the same kind of man.

The majority of wives told us that in spite of the problems that accompany being the child of a man at the top, their children loved and admired their father. Many fathers seemed able to pass on their drives and attitudes to their children in a way that was beneficial to them in the long run.

Madeline Lacovara, the wife of the former counsel to the Watergate Special Prosecutor and a mother of seven, told us about her three sons:

> *The boys have all incorporated the excellence ethic. They are fine students and enjoy competition. Our oldest son is in honors atomic physics at the University of Chicago, our second son is in pre-law at the University of Pennsylvania (he would like to be the same kind of lawyer that his father is), our third son is a history major at Harvard.*

A banker's wife wrote:

> *They already are following in his footsteps personality-wise. I imagine that they will choose different careers, however, because of different strengths and interests. My husband's success has given them opportunities, and they know it.*

Often children who have not been close to their father when they were young are able to communicate better with him as they get older. Some fathers enjoy their children more when they are grown up. Many women spoke of a new-found closeness between father and children after the teenage years.

In some families one child followed in his father's footsteps while the others went in very different directions. The mother of two sons said that this was the case in her family:

> *My older son is independently going his own way, refusing all financial aid from his dad, working as a machinist and supporting himself. My second son is like his dad in many ways and will probably pattern his life after his.*

Another woman made a similar statement about her daughters, two out of three of whom have become "third-generation bankers."

We also received some negative responses: Several women told us that their sons had no desire to work as hard as their father. Others said that their sons felt that they could never measure up to their father and didn't even want to try. A third group acknowledged that though their children wanted success, they didn't want to drive themselves as hard as their fathers had. They wanted to be able to spend more time with their families. Still others answered that their sons had chosen careers quite different from their father's so they wouldn't have to compete with him on his own turf. However, they had put similar amounts of time and energy into achieving their own success.

Perhaps the saddest reply to the question "Do you think your son(s) would like to follow in their father's footsteps?" came from the wife of an admiral, who wrote:

> *Our son believes that he can never attain the success of his father. He was successful only in drinking as much as his father, was hospitalized and is now with AA.*

We were labeled "sexist" by several women for separating the question into a son/daughter division and found that the majority of the daughters of men at the top wanted either a high degree of success for themselves or to marry men who were going to be successful—or both. The wife of one of New York's top publishers put it this way:

> *My daughters are well tuned to success and its hazards. Knowing the pros and cons, they will make their own decisions. I daresay they would prefer to be successful themselves rather than marry success. Perhaps they would like both.*

Shirley, the wife of a senior government official and the mother of three, had this to say:

> *I find this question sexist, perhaps because society still puts dads as role models for sons and mothers as role models for girls. I may sound a little defensive because I almost feel I am the role model for all my children, not just my daughters.*
>
> *My son does not identify with his father. If he did consider following in his footsteps, it would be for the gain of material things, not for admiration of his father's success. Instead, I see my oldest daughter unwilling to settle for less in life, enthralled with travel and meeting influential people, etc.*

In answering the question "Would you want your daughter to marry an ambitious and successful man?" the women surveyed often revealed their own feelings about marriage to such a man. The question allowed them to be completely honest without becoming dangerously personal.

Most said that they would want their daughters to marry such a man. Many said that their daughters already had. One asserted, "I can handle it, so she can too." Some frankly admitted they wanted their daughters to enjoy the material benefits of marriage to a man at the top. Charlotte, the wife of a Texas lawyer, put it more equivocally:

> *I would want her to marry a happy man with whom she is happy. If he is ambitious and successful, that's a lot better in my opinion than being a flake and a failure.*

Several other women replied that though they wanted their daughter to have financial security, they would rather she find someone who stressed family orientation and had a less demanding schedule than their own husband's. An executive's wife made an interesting comment:

> *My eighteen-year-old is dating a young man she wishes were more assertive, power oriented. Knowing the pitfalls, she still wants the excitement of life among the "doers."*

Jennifer, the politician's wife, told us:

> *If she chooses to, yes, but I would hope she'll marry a smart and ambitious man and will advance along with him in a successful career.*

The wife of a university president had mixed feelings:

> *Yes, but no one could be more ambitious, successful and driven than my daughters. I think both will be happy with live numbers, and I'll be there to pick up the pieces.*

But Michelle, the recently divorced diplomat's wife, definitely did not want her daughter to follow in *her* footsteps.

> *The worst thing she could discover about the person she falls in love with is that she will always be second, her wants, her needs,*

her dreams, her insecurities. They all look so disproportionately small and silly compared to the "real problems" men handle at work.

And finally here are the words of two women who represent opposite poles on this question. The older, somewhat bitter and resigned wife of a renowned professor was outraged. "Of course I'd want my daughter to marry an ambitious and successful man, wouldn't you?" she wrote. "What's better, a lazy good-for-nothing?" While Harriet, the thirty-five-year-old stockbroker's wife, stated firmly, "No, I hope she marries a shepherd."

Summing Up

Successful men often present difficult role models for children. Their jobs take them away from home for long stretches of time, and when they do come home, they are often tired and preoccupied. Their absences force a wife to play mother and father both, sometimes successfully, sometimes not. Often too she becomes a middleman, mediating between father and children. But the refusal of a wife to become a mediator can force a successful man to become more involved with his children and thus more successful as a father.

Guidelines

1. Try to help your husband to become aware of the effects that his success may be having on your children. His long hours away from home affect them, as does his attitude toward them when he is home.
2. Don't accept the role of mediator between father and children. An important part of parenting is the one-to-one connection between parent and child. Your husband and children can't make this connection with you in the middle.
3. Work on building closeness in the little time available for the family. Fathers, court your children. Children, spend time with your father even if it's just joining him on a trip to the hardware store.

3

CAREERS

Jean Sisco

Among the many women who participated in our survey, Jean was one of the few who combined a highly successful career of her own with marriage to an extremely successful man. During the years when her husband, Joe, was Undersecretary of State for Political Affairs, Jean rose through the ranks in her field of retailing and human resources. Now both are retired from their first careers and are partners in a new venture.

We interviewed Jean in the elegant Washington office which she and her husband share as consultants; she concentrates on the retail market in international trade, and Joe offers his expertise in country risk analysis to multinational corporations. Joe and Jean don't compete with each other; in fact, they spend far more time together than any of the other couples we interviewed. While we were talking to Jean, her husband called from a meeting at the State Department to ask her to check on the address of his luncheon appointment, which she cheerfully did. She then returned to the interview and a discussion of her own career.

Blond and fine boned, Jean looks younger than her fifty-six years, but when she talks, she speaks of herself as a pioneer:

When I wanted a business degree, only Stanford and the University of Chicago would accept women, and I was told that the only fields open to me were education, publishing and retailing. I chose retailing.

Joe and I met at Chicago when I was only nineteen. We had already graduated from college, and he wanted to get his Ph.D. and go into academia. I was determiend to have a career. All the women in my family had been career women, and I had strong role models in my mother and my aunt.

When Joe decided to work for the government, Jean came to Washington with him and immediately found a job in one of the large department stores in town. As he gradually moved into the political limelight, she rose higher in the store, earning twice as much as her husband but keeping a low profile in "official" Washington.

Jean continued to work while their children, two daughters, were growing up. She had originally planned to work part time after her oldest daughter was born, but gradually the job became full time again. She was personnel director of the company when she was pregnant with the second and feels that her bosses who allowed her to stay on were way ahead of their times. "Women just didn't go to work pregnant in those days," she said. "It wasn't considered proper."

Admitting that much of her salary went into child care, Jean also attributes much of her business success to having a husband who was supportive of her career and reinforced her decision to stay with it. "But I never expected him to manifest a great deal of interest in the world of retailing, just as I wasn't all that fascinated by foreign affairs," she asserted. What kept them together despite their sometimes divergent paths was the knowledge that they both gave their marriage priority. Jean told us:

You have got to decide how to do your career within the framework of your life-style. We put the marriage first, and I don't think this is a bad way to go. I've never felt deprived. And although his job was always demanding, when he was home, Joe helped with shopping, laundry and other household chores. He's a better cook than I am.

Joe's career has been a very public one, and sometimes I've been angry and really resented the things that have happened to him. But even though at times he might seem wrapped up in his work, I knew that if I ever said, "Damn it, this is important to me," he would do it. I knew that I had this kind of power, therefore I never had to use it. Just knowing that he'd quit for me was enough. I would never dream of asking him to.

Jean feels that she and Joe are a good team. From the point of view of their careers the team has required sacrifices from both, and she admits that each could have risen higher unencumbered by the other. But she believes that the sacrifices have been worth it. She is philosophical about the choices she has made:

I was a liberated woman long before it was fashionable, but I believe that to be a complete *woman, you should have a good marriage, children, and a career, in that order. And by a career I am not saying that it has to be commercial. I have a friend that I admire tremendously who is in charge of volunteers for the National Red Cross. She's never worked for money, but to me that's a career.*

I give a lot of talks to women's groups and get very turned off by all the young women who feel that a career is their only priority. If a woman wants a career, okay, but a career is many things. The pendulum has swung too far. I was made to feel less of a woman because I wanted to work when my children were school age; now women who don't really want jobs are forced out of the house as soon as the last child gets on the bus.

We asked Jean how she would advise other women who are married to hard-working, successful men. She felt that there were two factors to consider:

First of all, you have to have something that is your own. I don't care what form it takes, but it should be something you like to do, something you are good at, and something you value. If you have financial worries (which we had when my husband worked for the government), then you'd better find something commercial. If you are financially secure, then you can go into the arts, or into the community in other ways.

Secondly, choose something portable and universal, so if you move, you can take it with you, such as languages, computer sciences, writing, etc. You've got to be inventive, creative and flexible.

If you're going into a dual-career marriage, you had better know your strengths, and you'd better take advantage of them and be willing to compromise. You can have a traditional or a more unorthodox career, but you have to have the imagination and projection to plan for it. You don't just fall into it.

You don't make a career, whether it's a paid one or a volunteer one, overnight. I've been working on my career since I was sixteen.

The Generation Gap

The questions of whether or not to have a career, what form it should take and how much time should be devoted to it are ones that many women agonize over today. But when Jean was starting on hers, they were questions that were seldom asked. The women's movement has addressed itself to this issue perhaps more than any other. Sixteen-year-old girls now expect to grow up, have a career and live happily ever after, just as their mothers expected to grow up, get married and live happily ever after. But because the majority of today's young women will eventually marry also and bear children, pursuing a career successfully will always be a juggling act for them. Their lives are already far more fragmented than men's, and a career adds yet another variable. Combining a career with marriage to a man who is highly involved with his work is doubly difficult.

In this chapter we look at the question of careers from the point of view of the women we surveyed. We asked them what they had planned to do with their lives before they were married, whether they now had a career, and if so what difference that career had made to their marriages. Their answers very much reflected their age and the world they had grown up in. Eighty-seven percent of the women over fifty said no, they didn't have a career, while 79 percent of those under fifty were either pursuing a career at the present time or had worked in the past. Most of these careers were either traditionally women's professions, such as teaching, nursing and secretarial work, or some kind of creative or artistic venture. Also several women had free-lance businesses.

Two women we talked to typified the changing attitude of women toward themselves and their careers. The first, Cathy, was a twenty-eight-year-old editor in a major publishing house in Boston; the second, Phyllis, was the fifty-five-year-old wife of a professor and mother of four.

Cathy said:

> *When I got out of college, I had no idea of what I wanted to do, but I knew I wanted a career, and I had time to begin one. It was only by having a job I didn't like (secretarial) that I realized that unless I got some professional experience, I would always be someone else's assistant.*
>
> *My strategy is to get established in my career before I stop and have a family. That way if I take time off, I can pick up my career afterwards without starting all over again. Actually, I plan to hire someone to take care of the kids so I can keep my hand in with editing. The publishing world is a very social one; a lot depends on contacts. If I take too much time off, I'll lose the network I'm building up.*

Phyllis told us:

> *Right now I'm casting around for something for myself, but I don't really know what it's going to be. I have a real fear of getting into something too deeply and not being able to handle the pressure. But I feel guilty not having a job; everyone seems to have one these days.*
>
> *I love things that have to do with human behavior and psychology, but I don't have a degree, so I would have to go back to school. But I don't know if that's the answer because once I get the degree, I don't know what I'll do with it. . . .*
>
> *Jim is anxious for me to do something. I was almost enrolled for September, but I didn't do it. Now I think I'll wait until after my daughter's baby is born.*
>
> *I'm a little bit leery about my ability to do all these things. There are just so many burdens on my shoulders.*

Cathy's path seems to be the smoother of the two, although her attitude as well as future realities may change in unpredictable ways.

Certainly her plan is a good one, and her position is enviable. She is thinking about her career in terms that few older women ever have, and she is establishing herself professionally while she is relatively free to do so. However, marriage and babies may change her thinking dramatically. It may not be easy to be a superwoman, doing both, for a while, anyway.

In a cover story in the *New York Times Magazine* of November 21, 1982, several young mothers talked about the difficulties of juggling careers and children. Many of them have finally rejected the role of superwoman and feel that they must inevitably choose between the two. Some have switched to part-time work, thereby accepting lower pay as well as lower professional status. Others have dropped their careers completely.

The article points out that the idea of pursuing a career as well as being a wife and mother is a relatively new one and that the majority of women now attempting it do not have role models to follow. Unlike Jean, who acknowledged the influence of her mother and aunt, most of the career-minded women today did not have career woman mothers themselves.

Phyllis, on the other hand, looks at her own grown daughter and feels that she herself is missing something. "I really envy you doing this book," she told us. "I want to find a niche myself." But she is puzzled as to how to do that. She lacks professional skills, and more important, she lacks self-confidence. When Phyllis married, she had no thought of preparing for a career that she could pick up after her children no longer needed her undivided attention. She had never been under any kind of financial pressure to work, so she never had to. Now society is telling her she is missing something, and she wonders if it isn't true.

What Am I Going to Do When I Grow Up?

Almost all our participants, when asked what they had wanted to do before they got married, said "get married," and 65 percent, regardless of age, didn't question this priority. Angela's response was typical:

> *I planned to get married and to be the best possible wife and mother I could be, to share an interesting life with the man I loved. What more important aspiration and dream could there be?*

A senior military wife was more reflective:

> *A fifties girl had to be engaged shortly after her junior year in college and get married right after graduation or she would be a spinster all her life, a fate worse than death. This was the "ring by spring" mentality.*
>
> *Actually, I looked at a couple of career women and didn't like what I saw. None of us wanted to be like the old-maid professors at school. Being part of a loving team looked a lot more rewarding.*

Several of the older women had worked briefly after college but took jobs only to meet "Mr. Right." None of them seemed to have turned these early jobs into careers, and none planned their lives as Cathy has in order to have careers to return to after raising a family.

But some of these women did speak of other dreams and longings. "I planned to travel, have many affairs, and write love poetry," said one. "I was going to be a missionary in Africa," wrote another. Yet few of them had concrete plans for a career as did Jean, and most were ready and eager to seize Mr. Right's coattails when he came along.

More than one of the women who had wanted a career outside the traditional women's fields told us that she had been prevented from having one by her parents. Shirley, thirty-eight and now a psychiatric nurse, told us that she had originally wanted to be a doctor, but her father told her outright that he wasn't going to "put that kind of money into a girl." Her brothers were far better educated, she said. So she settled for the female side of the medical profession.

However, whether they had originally planned one or not, some of the younger women we surveyed said that they had a career now, while some of the older ones, like Phyllis, were searching for a "niche" outside the home. We will examine what some of these women had to say about their careers to find out whether pursuing a career is a plus or minus with respect to marriage to a successful man. And we will look for guidelines for coping with the special problems that dual-career families experience.

Parallel Lives or Collision Course?

A wife's career has a definite impact on her marriage. We found that many husbands expressed token approval of their wives' careers, but only so long as the work in no way interfered with the running of the house or the rearing of the children. Like many others, Jane, a thirty-five-year-old mother of five who had just gotten her Ph.D. in Chinese studies, told us that her husband had mixed feelings about what she was doing:

> *It's interesting to see the way he gives advice to young women in his office. He tends to be very supportive of these young professionals; he's been well trained by me.*
>
> *But when he comes home, it's "Great, you're studying Chinese, what's for dinner?" Larry couldn't have been more supportive of me writing the dissertation and would get mad if I goofed off or got behind, but he's never read the thing, and it's in English. It's sitting right there on the coffee table. But he brags to his colleagues about me. He acts as if it's a feather in his cap, as if he had a bright child.*

Just as different women have different feelings about their husbands' jobs, so men have different feelings about their wives' careers. In an article entitled "Ambitious Men, Can You Afford One?" (*Self* magazine, February, 1982) author Jane Adams asserts:

> *The big news is that today's striving young men frequently want women to have careers and interests of their own. They want you to take care of yourself so they don't have to. They don't want the responsibility for someone who lives her life vicariously.*

But many older men feel just the opposite. They seem to enjoy their wives' dependency and are proud of the fact that their wives don't have to work. Also they sometimes fear competition. "One superstar in the family is enough," said a well-known newspaperman. So there is often a feeling of conflict in younger wives who want to fulfill themselves in the older, more dependent pattern, and older wives who want more independence.

We feel that it is important for couples in two-career marriages, and those considering two-career marriages, to acknowledge and deal with the conflicting feelings that they both have. The more divergent their paths, the more they need to build bridges between them. Couples who are on collision courses are obviously headed for trouble, but couples who lead parallel lives can run aground, too. It would have made an enormous difference to Jane to have her husband read her dissertation even though he had no real interest in the subject. Knowing that he didn't would have made her even more appreciative because it would have been clearly an act of love.

As we consider the following six women and their careers, we will talk more about the dangers of collision courses, and the necessity for building bridges.

Karen: Government Analyst

Karen is an attractive red-haired civil servant. She is married to an American diplomat currently assigned to Washington. She herself works for another branch of the federal government and has done so for nine years. She said that her husband was "mildly interested" in her concerns but that he loved his own job and his satisfaction with it made him "a happier and more pleasant person to live with." Karen is thirty years old, has no children and is on a collision course with her husband. In rating her marriage, she gave it "perhaps a seven on a scale of ten," but as she talked about it, we concluded that it was precarious:

> My job gives me tremendous emotional and economic support, but I detest my husband's job. When Graham goes overseas again, I will stay here. One taste of embassy life abroad was plenty for me, thank you. My husband must accept this, or the marriage will dissolve.
>
> Our goals in life are completely different; he claims that I don't have any. His success gains him nothing that I want. Coping with

my husband's life is his problem, not mine. From that point of view my life is quite manageable.

I have determined to make no sacrifices. Any marriage re-quires compromise to survive, but sacrifice is a symptom of neuro-sis.

Karen is one of the new generation of diplomats' wives who have discarded an old role and taken on a new one. During the seventies many of the younger Foreign Service wives revolted against what they felt was the medieval mentality of the corps. In the old days a younger wife was completely at the mercy of senior wives, who required her help at parties and representational functions. If she refused, her husband's career would suffer. Now wives are officially "non-people" as far as their husbands' jobs are concerned. They can no longer be required to do anything they don't want to do, and they are beginning to respond to inner and outer pressures to have a career. But a career can be difficult for a diplomat's wife because of frequent international moves. Many marriages are breaking up be-cause of this. Do they have to?

What are Karen's alternatives? Must she choose between being a dependent Foreign Service wife on the one hand and a divorced career woman on the other? Keeping in mind Jean's advice to be creative and flexible, we believe that Karen's choices aren't so differ-ent from those of the other women we surveyed. Almost one third of the American population moves every five years, usually because of a husband's transfer or job change. Other working wives suffer dislocation, and many make compromises to keep their marriages alive. What makes Karen exceptional is her total unwillingness to compromise.

Karen acknowledges that she and her husband have different goals in life. She also admits that "any marriage requires compro-mise," but there is no evidence of compromise in her statements. Distinguishing between "compromise" and "sacrifice," she justifies doing neither herself. And yet she is asking her husband not only to compromise (settle differences by making mutual concessions) but to sacrifice his career for the sake of their marriage ("My husband must accept this, or the marriage will dissolve"). If sacrifice is a "symptom of neurosis," isn't she asking him to be neurotic? At no time does she show any understanding of his position. This is as vital a necessity in two-career marriages as it is in any other relationship.

Audrey: Psychologist

Audrey was one of the most remarkable and versatile women we interviewed. Soft-spoken and self-confident, she looked much younger than her thirty-nine years. She was married at sixteen and is the mother of seven. Her husband, John, is a lawyer, and she has recently become a career woman. She teaches psychology and works with heroin addicts in a county jail. She told us how she felt about her career and her family's reaction to it:

> *Working in the jail has been a wonderful experience. But when I started to work, I had to juggle between being a wife, mother, and career woman. I experienced a terrible, fantastic guilt. I can't even describe the amount of guilt I felt.*
>
> *When I was at work, I thought I should be home; when I was home, I felt I should be at work. I gave up sleeping almost totally for a year. I spent hours doing work at night so that I could jump up at six in the morning and cheerfully make five hundred pancakes and pack the kids' lunches and kiss them on their faces. Regardless of how fast I had to drive, I was always home when the kids came home from school.*
>
> *After about a year of that I said to myself, "I'm crazy!" so I went to see a friend of mine and said, "What am I doing wrong?" She said, "Slow down and size up the situation. You're trying to be perfect. Remember when you had a new white kitchen floor and how quickly you learned that the floor couldn't stay clean for long with seven pairs of feet running across it. Now think of your life in those terms."*
>
> *So I talked to the kids and said, "It's really a struggle for me to get back at three some days. I might be with a patient, and I feel very guilty leaving in the middle of it." They looked at me as if I were crazy and said, "Don't run home." The older ones took care of the little ones, and I began to relax. John enjoys my success*

and is grateful that I have managed my life, his life, and the children's lives.

An interesting thing happened recently. A very distressed patient showed up at my house one Sunday evening. I showed her into the living room and made sure everyone else left. We talked for a while, and then I took her to the hospital. Afterwards John was very upset that I wouldn't discuss the outcome of this case with him. Then I reminded him that when he had investigated a major political scandal, all I had gotten out of him was "no comment." At first he was a bit annoyed, then he thought it was funny.

Like many other women, Audrey had underestimated her children's adaptability. Once she communicated her feelings of guilt and frustration, they found a mutually workable solution. And by putting John in her shoes she helped him understand and accept her "no comment."

Harriet: Author

Although a very successful writer herself, Harriet approached us in distress. Her marriage to the chairman of one of Chicago's largest stockbrokerage firms was in trouble. Harriet writes books in her office in their large suburban home. Her books have sold well and have frequently been on the best seller list. Unfortunately her husband, Steve, doesn't approve of her career. His work world offers the only kind of success he can identify with, she told us:

He keeps quoting the fact that more than half of the women today are out in the workplace, but he doesn't consider my job a real job, just because I work at home. I feel degraded. At one point when he was involved with another woman from work, I asked him what she was like, and he said, "She's a lot like you, only successful." I've said time and again that if you judge a person's success by the location of her office or the title on the door, then we just go by different values. He'd like to see me in an office, but I'd die in an office.

Steve has never said that he's proud of my writing. It's very hard for him to give credit for things. I only earn two or three cents a copy on the books, and I have up to this year put all the money that I earn right into the common kitty. It didn't bother me because I thought, of course, marriage was forever. That actually gave him an opportunity to bring less money home and build up a little nest egg of his own.

Our marriage is a bit rocky now, and my lawyer said to keep what I earn, so now I have my own little nest egg, and Steve doesn't like it one bit. It's a sign of independence. Steve has often said that he wants me to be less dependent, but now that I'm showing independence, it doesn't sit well.

A wife's independence, financial or psychological or both, can be very threatening to a man, even though he thinks that's what he wants. As we have seen before, there seems to be a difference between the way a man see the career women he works with and the way he sees the wife he goes home to. One is extraneous and interesting, the other necessary and familiar. Sometimes he wishes his wife could be more like the women at work, who are usually younger, often better educated, and certainly more "modern." Perhaps Steve wanted Harriet to have an office so he wouldn't find "successful" women so attractive.

Since hard-driving, success-oriented men are necessarily highly competitive, it is often difficult for them to stop competing at home. Giving another person credit for something is difficult for them. One wonders whether Steve would really be proud of Harriet if she did get a "real job" or whether he would find himself competing with her even more.

The question of money, his and hers, comes up in every two-career marriage. Many wives do as Harriet did and pool their earnings with their husbands'. Expenses are paid out of a common account. Other couples divide their earnings into separate accounts from which he pays certain bills and she pays others. Several women we know who free-lance and earn modest amounts keep their money entirely to themselves, often using it to treat the family to something special or to buy things that they feel are essential but their husbands don't. One of the women we talked to who falls into this category said that she was very softhearted and had a hard time resisting a charitable cause. She felt it was unfair to use her husband's money for these contributions and loved having her own to give away.

The important thing about financial arrangements in two-career marriages is not how the money is divided or spent but that both people agree on how the money is managed. Here, as in so many other areas of marriage, communication and compromise are essential. If you feel it's unfair of him to build up a private nest egg while you're putting all your earnings into the common account, tell him. If he wants you to help put the kids through college instead of buying designer dresses, listen to him.

Sandra: Journalist

Sandra is the forty-five-year-old wife of an internationally known columnist and now a newspaperwoman herself. They have two children and make their home in Los Angeles, but her husband, Phil, spends much of his time traveling around the world. He is also much in demand as a speaker, "the lion of the lecture circuit," Sandra told us:

When I met Phil, I was very undirected. I traveled with him all over the world. It was an exciting time, and we met fascinating people, but for me it was unproductive. I loved having children, but even after they were born, Phil's career was still the center of my life. But while he was progressing, I was standing in the wings. Even when the kids were older and didn't need me so much, I still didn't have the courage to try something on my own. It was just too easy to ride the wave of his success.

Unfortunately I began to lose interest in what he was doing because I felt bitter about what I wasn't doing. Finally I went to journalism school myself and became more interested in his work again. I also began to take the possibility of working myself more seriously.

After I got my degree, I was afraid that I wouldn't get a job on my own, so Phil arranged for me to work in his office. This was a real turning point for me. I saw that other people who had jobs weren't really the supermen or superwomen I imagined. In fact, they weren't really any smarter or more capable than I was. And

sometimes they were scared too. That gave me a lot more confi-
dence.

I got my present job, a much better one, completely on my own.

The biggest obstacle to Sandra's success was her lack of self-confidence. This is often the case with women, especially those over forty,
who are married to very successful men. Comparisons are inevitable,
and it is always the women who come out looking inferior. And since
these women usually don't have to work, being married to such a
man can often seem like a career in itself. But we believe that every
person needs his or her individual success, whether financial or not.
Finding that you are as capable as everyone else in your own way
is very important. There is more to every woman's life than
housekeeping and child rearing, just as there is more to every man
than the job he holds.

Carol: Tutor

Carol, the blue-eyed forty-year-old mother of two, told us that the
turning point in her marriage to a New York executive came the day
he had lunch with David Rockefeller and Henry Kissinger. While he
was telling her about it over dinner, Carol couldn't help comparing
his lunch with hers, in the kitchen eating peanut butter with the kids.
"Eliot accused me of not being interested in what he was saying,"
she told us:

> *Of course I was interested—who wouldn't be? But I also began
> to feel cheated. I was just as smart as he was. Why had life dealt
> me such a different hand than it had dealt him? I think that a man
> doesn't have any idea of the fatigue and burnout of being with
> young children all the time. It's funny that it can be both exhaust-
> ing and boring, at the same time. Not that it's only boring, it's
> fascinating too. All of that is true.*
>
> *When the kids started in school full time, I decided to become
> a businessman(woman) myself. I figured the way to begin was to
> take the business boards. I did and did very well. Eliot was actually
> thrilled. He brought me a bouquet of yellow roses, something he
> hadn't done for years.*

Then, as I began to plan for my "brilliant career," I became aware of two things that I hadn't thought about before. One was Eliot himself. A lot of his success was the result of his tremendous energy and drive. He left the house early in the morning and came home long after the children were in bed at night. I just didn't have that kind of physical energy. My rhythm was slower and more contemplative. I was more attracted to the world of ideas than of action.

Also, once I considered turning the children over to the care of someone else, I found this very difficult. When I didn't feel so trapped anymore, I thought of how much fun they were to be with and how much I would miss by seeing them as little as Eliot did. And I had definite ideas of the kind of people I wanted them to be. No one else could bring them up the way I wanted them to grow.

At about this time I was offered a part-time job tutoring high-school students, and I took it. I loved the one-to-one contact, I loved teaching the older kids about history and literature. And I was home when my own kids needed me. Knowing that the other had been possible, that if I had really wanted to, I could probably have made it in my husband's world, made all the difference. I found out what I wanted to do by finding out what I didn't want to do.

Carol, like most of the younger women we interviewed, had gotten the women's liberation message, "Anything he can do you can do better," and much of her discontent was the result of society's changing values. "When you go to a dinner party and someone asks you what you do, you're not allowed to say, 'I'm a housewife,' " she told us. But some of her discontent came from within. She was bright and well educated. She and Eliot had met in college and had always been intellectual companions. But as he became more and more involved with his work, she threw herself into housekeeping and child rearing, and they grew apart. Her self-image suffered. "I was boring, even to myself. No wonder I felt boring to other people too," she said.

Like many other women, Carol first thought of following in her husband's footsteps when she decided to go to work. To many women this seems like the perfect way to combine career and marriage, and sometimes it is. A husband's work world is a familiar one —after all, he's been bringing it and work problems home for many years. But a husband's and wife's abilities are often very different, as Carol's and Eliot's are. Trying to force herself into her husband's mold will usually lead to a misfit for a wife. She has to find her own way, sometimes by process of elimination. Part-time jobs and volunteer work can be very helpful in this process.

Marion: Needlepointer

Still another angle on the question of a career was given us by Marion.

Fifty-one and the mother of four grown children, she is married to the president of a multinational corporation. Somewhat bitter about the role she is forced to play, she told us that it was impossible for her to have any life apart from her husband and his career:

> So you take some fascinating occupation—be it a job, a hobby, or an important volunteer position. You are supposed to and you want to be there. But no, you cannot tie yourself down to anything because your life is structured so that you must be available to drop everything and go with your successful husband on a business trip.
>
> You never know when the trip is coming up until a few days beforehand. You don't want to let other people in the organization down, so in the end you don't involve yourself in anything. You waffle around. Nothing is ever, therefore, fulfilling or steady. You dabble at this and that, accomplishing exactly nothing. If you do take on a job or whatever, there are arguments and friction with your husband so you just give it up, pack his suitcase (he doesn't have time), pack yours, close up the house, and you are on your way to be charming to his business associates.
>
> You should have a section in your book devoted to the popularity of needlepoint. Wives of successful executives often travel on business trips with their husbands. Sometimes frequently to the same city. The wife has seen all the museums, cathedrals, shops

and places of interest, so she stays in her hotel room most of the day with her loving, constant companion, the needlepoint canvas and thread. This makes her time pass until she has to dress up, make up and accompany her husband to a business dinner where she is his ornament. The most exciting thing that happened to me the last time I went with him overseas is that I met someone from my home town.

Martyrs and Choosers

In their book *Must Success Cost So Much?** Paul Evans and Fernando Bartolome divide the group of wives of the executives they interviewed into "martyrs" and "choosers." Although *martyr* seems a strangely inappropriate word to apply to Marion with her luxurious life-style, it is apt. Evans and Bartolome define a martyr as someone who waits until it is too late to launch a new life-style. "A lifestyle choice has been made without ever being chosen." The "chooser" on the other hand is one who "weighs the trade-offs between these and other life options and she commits herself one way or the other." They admit that choosing isn't simple and that the process can be a long one. The act of choosing, of taking responsibility for one's own life-style, can make all the difference. When Carol chose *not* to work full time, she found that she enjoyed her children much more. By wrestling with the options she ended up not far from where she had been before, but her attitude was entirely different. As long as Marion refuses to choose how she wants to live her life, she will feel trapped and unfulfilled. She could decide to get off the business-trip bandwagon, perhaps making her husband angry but for once quieting her own anger. She could compromise and go only sometimes, and find something to involve herself in at home in between. Or she could decide to make his trips her career, really getting below the surface in the cities they visit, learning the language if necessary, learning more about his business so that she wouldn't be just an "ornament" at his dinner parties. Perhaps she could turn her needle-pointing into a small business, as several of our partici-

*New York: Basic Books, 1981.

pants have. Her biggest problem is her attitude, and she has absolutely nothing to lose by changing that.

Volunteering

When Anne Spaak, the wife of the former ambassador from the European Communities, came to live in America, what impressed her most was how involved American women were in their communities. Actually American women are so used to giving their time to various causes that they seldom think about it. Few of them realize that volunteerism is almost unique to this country. The majority of women who participated in our survey were actively involved in volunteering at the time or had been in the past. Even some women with full-time jobs put in one or two evenings a week at a local hospital or civic organization. Seventy percent of our sample worked as volunteers in a variety of educational, social, political and religious organizations. Some did volunteer work in addition to having paid employment.

For most of these women volunteer work was beneficial and rewarding, enriching their lives and helping them acquire skills that sometimes translated into paying jobs. But few women did volunteer work in order to get "real" work. Most did it because they cared about their town, their school, their party or their church. This volunteering also helped them gain self-confidence and offered them a tremendous support system. We will talk more about support systems and their importance in Chapter 4.

Younger women who had school-age children said that they often helped out in the classroom, school office or library, on field trips or by chairing committees. Phyllis told us:

I have done lots *of volunteer work. At first it was out of the need to get away from my young children. I am very active in the PTA. This gives me a special satisfaction. It's sort of midway between staying home and having a career.*

You can have important responsibilities, meet people you have a lot in common with and get out of the house, and it's for the sake of the family. Children feel important when Mommy is the "boss" of some school event. Yet this can be overdone. Watch for the irony of neglecting your children in order to "help" them through school activities.

Many women had multiple volunteer responsibilities. A doctor's wife from Dallas wrote:

I'm a sociable person, and I like to get involved with those less fortunate than myself. I am all for women's causes, and I like to teach women to plunge ahead and use their skills and talents. I like to help those without education get an education or work. I like to read for the blind, shop for the elderly. I work part time, so I'm limited in this way, but I do enjoy giving.

Barbara Bush, who has done a great deal of volunteer work over the years, says that she is now concentrating on one project, "encouraging a proven program to help wipe out illiteracy. I am also helping raise money and volunteers for many different groups. My experience tells me that people who live for others are the happiest."

The wife of an attorney in Seattle works at a hospital for brain-damaged children, and a nurse works regularly as a volunteer with the Red Cross, doing blood-pressure screening and participating in health fairs. "It's volunteer work but in my field of expertise," she said. An executive's wife in Philadelphia takes her volunteer work very seriously:

It has been part of my life for twenty years. It's an 8 A.M. to 6 P.M., five-days-a-week job. I sit on fourteen boards and do special projects and committees with each. Often I am the only woman and currently chair a board that no woman has ever chaired. I'm sorry that women's lib denigrates this activity.

For many women, volunteer work is vital to their sense of well-being. In the words of one:

I need something to do in order to feel good. I think that this would be true for me even without a husband in the picture. I could never be just somebody's wife. I need attention for my accomplishments and like to do well, just like my husband does.

For wives of men who move often, volunteer work is often the easiest way of establishing themselves in a new community. The wife of a manufacturer told us:

> I have moved thirteen times. I have had so many volunteer jobs that you would be bored listening to them, but I was never bored doing them. I have worked with refugees, learning-disabled children, juvenile courts and drop-in centers for teenagers, and I have enjoyed it tremendously. I felt I could get to know various groups in society, learn different skills and work at a level appropriate to my situation at any given time.

Surely this woman is turning a negative aspect of her life—constant moving—into a positive one—learning new skills, finding out about her new communities. She would certainly fit Evans and Bartolome's definition of a "chooser." And in contrast to Karen, the diplomat's wife who refused to ever go overseas again, another wife of a Foreign Service officer said that she had found a whole new purpose in her life after her last tour abroad:

> I never went out for volunteer work per se, but in our last posting I had the opportunity to work in Vietnamese refugee camps, and this opened a whole new world to me. It was enormously rewarding and fulfilling.
>
> Now I feel that an essential part of life is to use one's time and energy and substance in the service of others.

Hearing women talk about their volunteer work in such terms made us aware of how valuable it is to them personally. This contrasted with the way many women talked about their paid jobs. With certain exceptions, Audrey and Carol, for example, most women who held paying jobs valued them for secondary benefits they conferred rather than as intrinsically rewarding. "It makes me more interesting to talk to," said a writer. "My job keeps me busy, so I don't miss my husband so much," wrote a teacher. "I'm more interesting to other men than I was when I was just a housewife," a businesswoman felt.

If a woman doesn't have to work for financial reasons, volunteer work is a good choice and often the choice that works best for the wives of very successful men. But recently it has been devalued, not by men but by women themselves. When women were kept out of the market place, they used volunteer work as a way of participating in the larger world around them. However, when being liberated came to mean being paid for work, volunteerism took on negative connotations. As long as women define success in terms of remuneration, they will be as trapped as they were when they defined it in terms of clean laundry and kitchen floors. All women should take their careers seriously, be they paid, volunteer or a combination of the two.

Summing Up

According to the *Oxford English Dictionary,* a career is "a person's course or progress through life," and in that sense all women have careers. Jean Sisco spoke of a career as a long-term choice of work, not necessarily financially rewarded but certainly planned for. She also said that her career had succeeded because she had made her marriage her first priority.

Without minimizing the difficulties of combining a career of any kind with marriage to a very successful man, we would like to point out that some women we interviewed were happier and more complete than others. Why? We believe it is because they had made their life-style a matter of choice, not necessity. Often they had turned necessity into choice, and by doing so they had stopped being martyrs and had become vital, fulfilled women.

Guidelines

Looking back on this chapter, we can point to certain positive ways of coping with both a career and marriage to a successful man.

1. Find out what *you* want to do and like to do. Decide whether money is important. Be flexible; you'll probably have to move your career around. Plan ahead and stick with it. A career is a long-term commitment.
2. Build up your self-confidence by approaching your career as a series of stepping stones. Don't compare yourself when you start

out with people who have already arrived. Little successes lead to bigger successes.

3. Don't be a martyr. It's bad for your health and your marriage. Size up your situation, be realistic about your options and make a choice about your life-style. Don't be afraid to choose; you can change your mind, but don't avoid choosing. And don't wait. The time to take yourself seriously is now. Nobody was born to be another person's ornament.

4. If you're on a collision course with your husband's career, get off, unless you enjoy pain. If you're leading parallel lives, build bridges.

5. Try to walk in your husband's shoes sometimes. Don't expect him to make sacrifices that you wouldn't consider making. Remember that compromise involves mutual concessions.

6. Don't underestimate your children. They can adapt to changes in their routine if you spell out the problems and involve them in the problem solving.

7. No matter how different your career is from your husband's, you can always find things in common to connect the two. Sharing is bridge building. Communicate!

8. Work out your financial arrangements together. It's not as important what they are as it is that they be mutually satisfactory. Here again communication is essential.

9. If you're not happy staying home, find out why. Are you just discontent because other people tell you you should be. Don't misfit yourself into someone else's career just because it's handy. Find out what *you* really want.

10. Consider volunteering as a fulfilling career. Many women have found as much satisfaction in being a volunteer as in paid employment.

4

FRIENDS

Louise

Like almost all the wives of successful men whom we questioned, Louise told us that friends were very important to her. They constituted one of her support systems. We will discuss the importance of friends, family and other support systems in this chapter. We will also point out some of the problems wives at the top have in making and keeping friends and the inevitable loneliness and alienation that result. At the end of the chapter the reader will find guidelines to help her cope with loneliness and build up her own support systems.

Louise is the lovely but troubled wife of a Midwestern politician. She had suffered several bouts of depression and, a year before we interviewed her, had tried to commit suicide by overdosing on tranquilizers. Now on medication and under the care of a psychiatrist, Louise feels that she is on the road back to normalcy. She talked to us on the porch of her large white house; sipping iced tea, she seemed composed and at peace. But what she said had dark undertones:

> *I can't blame my brain chemistry on anybody. I was born this way. What I can say is that people who are depressives find certain situations difficult, like a husband who is always telling you how much he loves you but who spends fifteen to sixteen hours a day at the office for years and years and years. This provides an atmosphere for depression to flourish.*
>
> *When I started to get better, I began to look at my friendships and realized that I was really demanding too much from my*

friends. I felt people drawing away from me, and one day I woke up and said to myself, "You're relatively lucky. You've got a terrific shrink. You can tell him anything twice a week, and not everybody's that fortunate. Snap out of this! You need your friends to be friends, not amateur psychiatrists. Be able to be lighthearted and have some levity in your friendships. Be able to go out to lunch and have a nice time without talking about how badly you feel all the time."

I was doing it all wrong, and I knew I was. So I called everyone and said that from now on it was going to be different. One friend still asks me sometimes how things are going, but I say, "Sally, remember my phone call? If I need to tell you something, I will, but I can do without talking about it right now."

Often left alone by their busy husbands, the wives we talked to relied heavily on their friends. This was particularly true of women who had moved from their home towns to live in another, often larger city. Those who stayed closer to home also relied on their families for support. For those who had moved, friends became like an extended family.

Louise had grown up in a small town in the South but had moved away when she married. For many years she felt that she had outgrown her friends back home. In her view these women had taken the easy way out by marrying childhood sweethearts and living down the road from their parents. When discussing this, she told us about her attitude toward her old friends:

I had developed a mental picture of their simple lives in the suburbs with nine-to-five husbands and children who looked like the kids on the box of cornflakes. I pictured them doing volunteer work for the Junior League and eating chicken salad at the country club.

Last winter I went back home to see a dying aunt, and while I was there, I saw some of my childhood friends. Two had been deserted by faithless husbands, one [left] with the responsibility of raising four children (three of them triplets) and the other with a retarded child. Another friend still had her husband, but her daughter had anorexia nervosa.

These are courageous women who lead complicated lives and are succeeding at it themselves. I realized that I have by no means "outgrown" them. I just have a different set of problems to deal with, that's all.

During the years that Louise had spent away from home, she had met interesting people, expanded her horizons and broadened her own outlook on life. This was threatening to some of her old friends, who felt that she had changed completely and would no longer be interested in them. She told us that she had had to reach out more to them, to be the one to make the first overture.

But although Louise had developed and grown away from her old friends to some extent, she was still a small-town girl inside. When she married, she had had a hard time feeling comfortable with her sophisticated new friends. "I fell between two stools," she told us:

This was my neurotic problem. I didn't feel equal to many of the other women in our social group. They were richer, more sophisticated and generally very different from me. I think that it was hard for them to identify with me or me to identify with them.

I knew that there were women like me squirreled away somewhere, but I had to go out and hunt for them. I could always spot them because they were the women whose nails weren't manicured.

Now I have many friends here in all walks of life. But before I worked on the problem, I found myself in social situations where establishing friendships was difficult; so many relationships based on professional contacts are superficial and fleeting. And so much of the socializing that my husband and I do is politics.

Louise's experience is a common one for many wives at the top. Moving away from home town and friends and establishing new support systems is never easy, and her mental condition made it even more difficult for her. Because her mental health problems were serious, Louise needed the professional support of a psychiatrist. After she had regained her equilibrium, she restructured her friendships. Reestablishing ties with old friends and revising her approach to new ones helped her recovery. Despite the glamorous public life of a politician's wife, Louise still needed friends very much. Almost all of the women we questioned said that this was true of them too.

Loneliness

Seventy-eight percent of the women we questioned agreed with the statement "It's lonely at the top." Of those who agreed, some said that they were lonely because their husbands were away from them for so much of the time. Others told us that they were lonely because their husbands' positions made it difficult for them to make friends. Many had both problems. Those women who disagreed with the statement maintained that it could be lonely but that it didn't need to be; that it all depended on your attitude.

We found it interesting that a number of our participants, including the wife of a Senator and the wife of one of the country's top executives, did not feel that they were "at the top" and said so. They then went on to say what they thought they would feel if they had been at the top. On the other hand, the wife of a fisherman could relate to the question because, as she said, "Our small-town society puts us at the top."

One cause of loneliness was having a husband who worked long hours and came home late. The women who said they were lonely primarily because of their husbands' long hours tended to be older women (over fifty) who admitted to having few or no support systems. "I have no support system at all," said Martha, the fifty-five-year-old wife of a banker:

> My lonely times are when I don't have a husband to share with or to look forward to being with. My husband spends his time and energy on his job.
> It's mainly lonely because I don't have my man. Even though I am very busy with the house and all, I don't feel I am really living with and sharing my life with my husband. I married for companionship, but it hasn't worked out that way.

Martha went on to admit that she sometimes smarts at "bringing up the rear with no identity of my own."

However, most women told us that they had a hard time making friends and that made them lonely. People tended to set them apart because of their husbands' positions. This led to isolation. Those who did approach them often seemed to be social climbers trying to ingratiate themselves, also because of their husbands' positions. Typical of these women were Maria, the diplomat's wife, and Eileen, who is married to a Senator.

Maria said:

> *I think people treat you differently when you're "at the top."*
> *When we were last overseas, my husband was an ambassador. I*
> *didn't realize it at first, but people just expected me to be a snob,*
> *which is the last thing I would ever want to be. I wasn't a snob*
> *before he became ambassador—why would I become one after his*
> *appointment? But since these women hadn't known me in my*
> *blue-jean days, it was hard to overcome the barriers.*
>
> *I was really unhappy that his job made it very hard for me to*
> *make friends in the embassy. I needed friends as much as I ever*
> *had, which was very much. I hadn't changed, only my husband's*
> *position had, and I was being penalized for it.*
>
> *And there was another problem. I couldn't get really friendly*
> *with the other women because of jealousy among them. No one*
> *invited me over for a cup of coffee for fear that the others would*
> *think that she was trying to butter me up.*
>
> *We've been in the Foreign Service for almost twenty years, and*
> *I've never met a happy ambassador's wife. Now I know why.*

Maria was very outgoing and refused to remain friendless. Eventually realizing that she had to look outside the embassy for support, she found that other ambassadors' wives were feeling lonely too, and this established a common bond between them. She also involved herself with local people who were completely unconnected with the embassy. "I didn't talk about who I was, and since I didn't they soon forgot about it and really responded to me as an individual," she said. But Maria and her husband were caught up in a very demanding official social life which took time away from developing those new friendships:

> *The business social functions we went to are actually work. I*
> *never went anticipating meeting anyone who could be a buddy. I'm*
> *not saying it couldn't happen, but I wasn't looking for it. I'm*

realistic enough to realize that if we were invited to those dinners, it wasn't because of my sparkling personality or even my husband's. It's because of the power he wields or is perceived to wield. That's what gets us invited.

Eileen experienced many of the problems Maria did, and a few others as well. Living in Washington but keeping close ties with the state her husband represents, Eileen had two completely different sets of friends:

The ones at home don't understand our life in Washington; the ones in Washington don't understand our life at home. Sometimes I feel split in two, but other times I'm glad that I have a special perspective on both. But the truth is, I don't really belong in either. I lead a double life.

Jealousy

Jealousy was also a problem for Eileen as well as many other women we interviewed. Old friends envied her position and her husband's prosperity:

People look at you differently and envy you. They watch you closely. How many people have the opportunity to go in and out of the White House and talk to a president. Not many. There are only a few dozen people in the whole world that do what my husband does. When you look at it from that side, it's very special.

But Eileen contended that the glamour and the "benefits" of her life are mostly in the eye of the beholder:

It's not as if there were really so many doggone benefits anyway. When congressional wives get together, it's such a joke. We know how prominent and powerful our men are, but that power is really illusionary, except for a few superstars, and even they have to worry about the next election and losing it all overnight. So there isn't that much to envy from the inside.

Because my husband is also a lawyer, we're doing better finan-

*cially than some of our old friends, and jealousy comes in here too.
I do feel guilty with some of them.*

*I try hard not to act any different, but I worry about the
impression people may get if they find out that we can afford
certain luxuries. I almost would rather do without something than
have my friends feel uncomfortable.*

*I was embarrassed when we bought a new car back home
because of what the neighbors would say or think. One of them
came up and said: "It must be nice to have money."*

*It's lonely because everyone thinks that you have everything
and that money solves all problems. Unfortunately, when some
people reach the top, they assume an attitude of superiority, and
this too leads to envy. It is hard to maintain an image that you
are still the same kind of caring person. Often people won't accept that. That's why it's lonely at the top. Too bad, because it
should be fun.*

Yes, It Can Be Lonely, But . . .

The attitude of superiority that Eileen spoke of seems to be an
important contributor to loneliness. In his book *Loneliness Is Not a
Disease,* Tim Timmons* says that loneliness is a decision. He maintains that it's a natural law, like the law of gravity, that if you give
of yourself to other people, they will give back to you. All the women
who said that they weren't lonely agreed with this statement. Dottie
Blackmun wrote:

*Since age twenty-six, I have known exactly who I am and
where I stand. I am an extremely friendly person with no pretenses,
on a level with everyone from the custodial help to the head of any
government in the world. I find good in almost everyone.*

A bishop's wife told us:

*Having met persons who have become more concerned with
material things than with people as they have climbed up the
ladder of success, I make a conscious effort to be down to earth*

*New York: Ballantine Books, 1981.

> *with all whom I encounter. I find this posture generally breaks the ice and we get along very well.*
>
> *If you are wearing a mask at the top, you will be lonely there. If you are genuinely yourself, you will attract others. If you take time to reach out, you will receive in return. The lonely ones are usually afraid to be themselves at the top.*
>
> *It's important to remember who you are inside and where you came from. Don't ever forget that, and remind others if they forget. Don't forget where you started.*

Audrey made another important point:

> *I consider that every adult human being is alone. Whether or not one is lonely depends on one's inner resources. The demarcations are simply clearer at the top. But wherever you are, that place is what you make of it. If you allow yourself to be lonely, then you will be.*
>
> *It's lonely for some, for those who have allowed ambition to isolate them from real relationships. Wealth and success don't inevitably lead to loneliness. Loneliness is a personality problem of an individual's own choosing.*

It's My Husband's Problem

Louise Bernikow wrote an article for the *New York Times** on the subject of loneliness. She quoted psychiatrist Dr. Sol Landau, who says that the loneliest people he sees are men, specifically workaholics who put all their mental and physical energy into their jobs. Although Bernikow says in her article that women admit to being lonely much more often than men do, men very often suffer from this condition too.

Twenty-five percent of our respondents mentioned their husbands in answering our question about loneliness, but we have no way of knowing whether their husbands would have admitted to being lonely. The wife of the CEO of a large manufacturing company put it this way:

*August 15, 1982.

I'm not lonely. I think that this is a question you should address to the person at the top, not his spouse. My husband has to be careful in that the guys he used to work for now work for him. He can no longer confide in them as before, and I feel that he has lost out in that way.

In relocating, most people find friends within the organization, but being boss makes this impossible. His employees feel uneasy with him socially. He has few people to turn to for luncheon engagements because his staff is reluctant to ask the boss to join them. He really misses out on the camaraderie lower down.

Also, if he did have friends with whom to share his success, would they be happy for him? I sincerely doubt it!

The intensely competitive work environment of a successful man acts as a non-support system. Of necessity competition separates and isolates. The man at the top can't confide in business associates because they can't understand his problems, because of the need for confidentiality and because anyone he talked to would naturally wonder how the boss's decisions would affect him.

Before writing *The Wonderful Crisis of Middle Age,* Eda LeShan interviewed hundreds of men and women. She had this to say in her chapter entitled "The Oppression of Men, by Themselves":

It may well be that men get paid better salaries and are not discriminated against by colleagues and employers, as women too often are, but I must admit I've come to see their lives as even more oppressed than women's. Women tend to be more aware of themselves and their problems; they feel their fears and their angers very openly and they are constantly examining and reassessing their lives.

My conversations with men have led me to the conclusion that men are less flexible, and are far more defended against expressing their feelings. . . .

Another problem for the middle-aged man is that he tends to carry the burden of emotional isolation from other men. He may have dozens of male acquaintances but rarely a real friend, the kind his wife has. . . . There are exceptions of course, but my impression is that on the whole, men tend to have relatively superficial relationships with other men. Friendships tend to be with the husbands of their wives' friends. Most of the men I talked to looked surprised when I asked if they had any really close men friends, with whom they shared their sorrows, or worries or deeper feelings. . . . One candid fellow said, "You know, I have the feeling that many middle-aged affairs occur because a man is looking for a friend and he doesn't know how to find or be a friend with another man."*

Highly successful men work so hard that they have little time for casual socializing outside the office. Their long hours would not give them time to cultivate real friendships even if they wanted them, and usually their single-mindedness keeps them from socializing with people from different backgrounds. "He's not interested in anyone who can't talk business," said one woman. These men get little social reinforcement outside of work, and they put all their energies into their work, where they get none at all. This seems to be a real vicious cycle but one that a wife can help break if she overcomes her own loneliness and builds up her own support systems.

Support Systems

The existence of a support system, be it in the form of family, friends, colleagues, organizations or religious faith, proved invaluable to those women who had one. The need to confide in someone sympathetic was particularly strong in younger women with small children, women whose husbands traveled frequently, and women, like Louise, who had serious psychological problems. Several older women said that they didn't need a support system and were doing just fine without one.

Some women whose husbands were in positions of high visibility told us that although they would have liked a more extensive support system, this was discouraged by their husbands. Others hesitated to "unburden" themselves to anyone outside their family because they feared that this would compromise their husbands' status or career. An executive's wife told us:

Corporations do not make for warm, secure support groups, so I felt uneasy but didn't know why. I had it all, so I couldn't understand what my problem was.

*Eda LeShan, *The Wonderful Crisis of Middle Age* (New York: David McKay Company, 1973), p. 95.

Looking back, I do understand. It's the nature of a competitive situation, not my husband, or his boss, or anyone. I could have been happier if this knowledge had gotten through to me. I was happy on the outside but not on the inside.

Mildred, the seventy-five-year-old wife of an enormously successful businessman, considered by all to be a real pillar of society, finally left her husband after fifty years of marriage. She talked to us about her support systems:

My brother and two sisters—who knew over the years how unhappy I was with my husband—gave me loving support, which I appreciated. I was careful not to let my unhappiness with my husband be known outside the family and did not talk to our minister. He would have reported to my husband, and matters would have been worse for me.

Keeping up appearances that all is well often makes it impossible for wives to get the support they need. Some women complained that their husbands didn't want the wives in the company talking to one another. They were afraid that it would somehow reflect negatively on them. Janet, one of the women who asked to participate in our survey, told us:

My friends were fascinated when I read the questionnaire to them, but one, who is the wife of a financial consultant, told me that her husband would never let her participate in something like this.

I think that there is a real need for your book. I've tried to broach some of these questions with other women in my husband's company, but many of them will not admit that there's any problem at all; most of them repress it. I've made the mistake of trying to talk to them, and it's been very awkward.

And the husbands don't want their wives to be involved with each other. The CEOs I've met who have been of my husband's vintage (sixty) don't want their wives friendly with each other, so wives were very nervous about this. They have been programmed.

The need to keep personal problems within the family made some women turn to their husbands for support. Angela, the wife of the

CEO, said that she and her husband are a mutual support system out of necessity. She feels that this has helped them develop a close relationship. "But," she adds, "even though I can cry on his shoulder, he really can't cry on mine. He finds it hard to share his feelings."

Many of the women who said that their main support came from their husbands were over sixty. They had adjusted to the unique demands of being married to successful men, and many reported that they did not need a support system at all. Wilma, the sixty-two-year-old wife of a publisher, wrote:

Most of the time I am so busy I don't have the time to think about what support systems I need. Reading, learning, family and long conversations with my husband are my support system.

Reading, learning and family in particular can certainly provide excellent support. Fifteen percent of the women we interviewed said that they got support from their children. (All these women fell into the "over fifty" category.) Thus, they kept their confidences within the safe circle of the family. Also, no matter how many cross-country or international moves they made, these ties were not likely to be broken. The forty-two-year-old wife of an attorney and mother of five said:

My two oldest girls are my best friends. My supportive mother, at seventy-four, is still very much around. I have several close girl friends who think I am the luckiest, busiest, happiest person they know.

An architect's wife and mother of two sons told us:

I am close to my sons. I talk to them a lot, probably when I should be talking to my husband. They listen! They talk to me also, rather than my husband.

A close relationship between parent and child can supplement relationships with peers. Obviously it is ideal to have both. Also jealousy was sometimes a problem with other relatives. Sometimes brothers and sisters compared their situation with their sibling who had married success and felt anything but supportive.

FRIENDS

For most women who had support systems outside of the family, these consisted of friends: usually other women. But while some became friendly with women from all walks of life, others felt it was more comfortable and easier to develop friendships with people in similar circumstances. Eileen felt this way:

> *There are only a few people who understand that there are sacrifices that you make to "make it," and even then it isn't easy. I feel uncomfortable, for instance, griping about the cost of anything because other people have much more right to gripe than I do. You must not show off or hurt others by your success.*

And Peggy said that her only support system was friends "in the same boat."

> *It's hard to make close friends in political circles. I moved to Washington with my husband after the elections. It took a long time, but I've finally met people who are my supports, other political wives.*
>
> *It has really helped me to get to know other women in similar situations and to learn how they cope with their husbands' success, retain their own identities and pursue achievements of their own.*

Sally, the forty-year-old wife of a self-made businessman, also had trouble when she moved to a new city:

> *I need support systems and feel them lacking. I've had friends who helped me cope. These were other young wives waiting for "him" to come home for dinner.*
>
> *During one five-year period I had four relationships with men, not sexual, but real companionships. They were people to talk to, not recipe and baby talk but real conversations. These were men we both knew within the organization who, when traveling from the various offices across the country, would take me to dinner, my husband being also on the road. These nights out provided me with my own identity. They were with our spouses' knowledge and*

"permission" and provided support for both myself and the men. They were real friendships because the men were free.

It is very difficult to get out with other wives whose husbands are home every night. I often found that I was too tired to struggle finding a sitter and getting dressed up just to go to an organizational meeting of some sort, so I didn't join any organizations. Arts and crafts classes got very boring, but they did get me out of the house during the day.

I do not have strong friendships here in New York, though I did have them in the Midwest. Relationships here are very superficial. Everyone is fighting to get ahead, and close friendships are hard to come by.

On the other hand, Jane, whose five children are under ten, depends very much on other women with young children:

I find that having close women friends, usually mothers of similarly aged children, is extremely important. Men don't always nurture close friends; too busy being competitive against other men.

Women aren't afraid to talk over problems or to admit "I can't do anything with my kids!" Chances are the friend knows exactly how you feel and can offer some advice, or at least consolation.

It's very important to maintain old and new friendships like this and to remind your husband that an evening with old "real" friends can sometimes be more valuable than an evening with new "contacts" or people he wants to impress.

Having friends not related to one's position or career gives a person a release, a chance to relax without having to worry about saying or doing the right thing. Also such friends help a person to maintain a balance in life. It keeps you from becoming too self-centered or taking yourself too seriously.

Moving, sometimes after only a few years in one location, often makes friendships a problem for women married to upwardly mobile men, as it does for almost anyone who moves. One woman who has recently moved said:

We do not live near family, so friends become like family. But it's difficult to pour out your guts to a neighbor you've only known

a couple of months. You don't want to tell a new friend all of your
problems and scare her away. Deep friendships take time, and in
our community no one lives near you that long. Either she moves
away, or you do.

I just call an old friend in California when I really need
support, even if it's daytime rates. It's cheaper than a shrink.

Sometimes it is difficult for women to connect their husbands
with their friends, especially if their friendships are made outside the
husband's organization, as many are. In spite of what Eda LeShan
says (A man's friends tend to be the husbands of his wife's friends),
we found that with wives of successful men the situation seemed to
be reversed. These women often felt most comfortable with the wives
of their husbands' associates, unless their husbands discouraged it.
The second strongest support system mentioned was old or childhood friends; the third was friends with whom the women shared an
interest, such as children, hobbies, or activities; and the fourth was
professional friends of their own.

Although most of the women we surveyed seemed to adapt themselves readily to their husbands' social demands, it was often hard
for the husbands to fit in with their wives' friends. Jennifer, the wife
of a congressman, decided to keep her own name after she married,
and few of her own friends cared who her husband was. She told us
that he was very uncomfortable with this lack of recognition at
parties where everyone knew her. He was used to being the center
of attention. As she described it:

Everybody came up to me and talked to me, and nobody spoke
to him. He just sat there like a bump on a log and looked gloomy.
I asked him, "What's the matter, honey?" and he said, "I feel like
a fifth wheel."

I reminded him that that was what I feel like when I go to his
parties and nobody pays any attention to me.

Jennifer said she not only enjoyed the support of her own friends,
they also helped her to keep her husband's world in perspective. She
felt that he needed to be reminded that he wasn't always number one,
that no one was. He also needed to see that his wife was appreciated
for herself, and not just as an extension of him.

Because the average age of the women who participated in our study was over forty, most of the wives we interviewed were not currently working. But a large minority were, and for them the greatest support system was without a doubt their co-workers. Many working women told us that their strongest ties outside the family were with the people they worked with, men and women. Here the wife of a successful man could feel successful in her own right. Here were people who relieved her of the burden of wearing a mask as "the wife of . . . " Here were people who were interested in her concerns because they shared them. And thanks to their support she was able to be more understanding and supportive herself.

ORGANIZATIONS

A variety of organizations and social groups have proved to be of immense benefit to the women we talked to: NOW, the U.S. Jayceettes, the Junior League, Overeaters Anonymous, AA and Bible study groups were mentioned often. So were courses at local colleges, and civic organizations. An annotated list of helpful groups will appear in Chapter 8: "Resources."

Bonnie-Jean shared her enthusiasm about support systems with us:

I've always needed support systems because we've never lived close to any family members. I've used my local alumnae group and the Junior League of the area. Wherever we are, I ask women what they do with the time outside the home and carefully select an organization I'm interested in. As a member of an organization I know how delighted we are to find a new member. I've never had any trouble getting involved.

But I learned early on that I've got to be the one who makes the effort to find the groups. Persistence pays off. Otherwise, I'd be home alone waiting for the phone to ring, and it won't.

For Angela organizations took the place of close friendships as sources of support. She wrote:

I have a number of good friends, but no single best whole friend. I am a very private person and don't share myself with any

*one person. I've learned over the years of my husband's career that
I must be careful what I say. I've had my trust betrayed once or
twice, and I am wary of what I tell anyone.*

Women who can't find organizations that interest them sometimes start their own. Nina, a writer, told us that she had done this:

*After a marital crisis we moved, leaving all our friends in
Massachusetts, where we had lived for ten years. I needed help but
didn't know where to find it in our new community. So I founded
two journals that are still in existence. One was for women in crisis,
and one for men who had served in Vietnam (as my husband had
done) who were experiencing "delayed stress syndrome."*

*These publications have put me in touch with many men and
women who are experiencing crises and are trying to work their
way out. Not only does it give me personal support, but I feel that
I am helping others.*

And MaryJo, the wife of a doctor, found her greatest support in
a group that she helped assemble:

*In St. Louis my support system was definitely centered on our
church. Here in Houston my support is a group with a common
interest in "Life in the Spirit." It is not really connected with the
church itself.*

*I have learned over time how to make close friends. It takes
a lot of loving, giving, and time.*

PROFESSIONAL SUPPORT

Some women, like Louise, needed the support of a doctor or psychiatrist. Often this meant long-term care until they recovered their
mental health. Others used professional treatment or counseling
from time to time to deal with personal or family crises. Michelle,
the attractive wife of a diplomat stationed in South America, was
desperate for help when she discovered her husband's infidelity, but
it was very difficult for her to get treatment:

*Several years ago Greg confronted me with the fact that he had
a mistress and had almost left me for her. This was the beginning*

of the end. He also told me he had no regrets, no guilt, and wasn't going to change.

I tried to deal with it alone for a year. I was close to suicide, and finally he let me try to get some help. But it couldn't be done in the capital because of his precious career. He had me travel to the next-biggest town (a two-hour drive each way) once a week so nobody would know about it. I had to do it in hiding. Regaining my self-confidence has taken me about ten years.

Michelle and her husband are now divorced, and she finds that she has far more friends than she did while they were married.

Some women with less serious problems and more accommodating husbands mentioned they got support from their priest, pastor or rabbi or a local mental-health center.

Summing Up

The majority of the women we interviewed said that family, friends and other support systems were important in helping them to cope with the problems of being married to very successful men. A few older women said that they had no support systems and believed that being self-sufficient was more important than finding support. They advised, "Just get ahold of yourself!" But most women needed friends especially and also recommended various groups and organizations as support systems. They acknowledged that they had to be the ones to initiate their friendships because their husbands' success had put them in an "elevated" position.

Perhaps the saddest reply to our question about support systems came from Joanne, who said:

Unfortunately, I have no support and therefore feel a deep sense of desperation sometimes. I feel that no one really knows what is going on. On the surface everything seems "rosy," but no one knows the real situation.

Guidelines

1. "Make new friends, but keep the old; one is silver, and the other's gold."
2. Go out of your way to cultivate relationships with old friends and others who are not part of your husband's successful world. Call them up, invite them out, don't brag or act superior. Don't wear a mask unless you want to play a part.
3. Try also to make contact with women who are "in the same boat." It helps to share feelings with people who can identify with your problems.
4. Look for clubs, groups or organizations that offer something that you need. If you don't find the right one, consider starting one of your own.
5. Don't lean on friends or family for really serious problems. If you're chronically depressed or feeling suicidal, get professional help. Try your minister or rabbi or call your local crisis center for information on where to go for help. Also, check our list of resources at the back of this book.

5

OUTER STRESSES

Roscoe Dellums

In this chapter we will discuss what we call "outer stresses." These are outside pressures which wives of successful men experience because of their husbands' jobs or positions. Like many other wives who would be considered at the top, Roscoe Dellums experiences certain stresses that are unique: social demands; living in the public eye; having to share her husband with admiring and not so admiring constituents. We interviewed Roscoe, who had just taken the Washington, D.C., bar exam, in her Chevy Chase home. Petite and dynamic, she was dressed in a black velvet pants suit designed by her husband, Ron. She admitted that their marriage, obviously a strong one, has suffered at times from the stresses of his job. She told us about some of these stresses and how she has handled them:

> *These men are under enormous pressure, and many times things that happen are not prompted by them. The closer people get to power, the stronger the temptations are. It's incredible how power, or just the semblance of power, is enough to attract.*
>
> *There is nothing other than giving birth that has any similarity to sitting up waiting for that vote. You are about to sell your soul and say, "Oh, please, let him win!" The hardest thing is to lose those elections. That is devastating. Nobody wants to be a loser.*

Roscoe, like many other wives in the public eye, has mixed feelings about the press. She feels that it considers her husband, who is also black, as important only when it comes to black issues. "The world is not just divided into black and white," she said, and she wishes that the press would approach her husband as more of a generalist. She went on to say:

> *We really lead a fish-bowl existence. The press watches every-*
> *thing we do, especially if it gives them some gossip to report. But*
> *things have really changed since the Ninety-second Congress. We*
> *were in this group of congressmen who were getting their divorces*
> *in the middle of a re-election campaign, and the electorate was*
> *getting used to it. It wasn't an obstacle anymore. Before you had*
> *some leverage. You knew these men didn't want any scandal*
> *during an election year.*
>
> *When people hold certain positions, they become a focal point.*
> *Society is always interested in the negative stuff because that is*
> *what the media feeds them, it sells newspapers. But really I find*
> *the members of Congress as a group very dull. Their wives, well,*
> *they're nice people, but none of us is worth envying. We're not*
> *really a group worth monitoring.*
>
> *Sure you have these scandals, Abscam, the Jenerettes and the*
> *allegations about my husband. But whenever you aggregate well*
> *over five hundred people, one can always find a few rotten apples*
> *if that's what one is searching for in the barrel. People think that*
> *we're always having swinging parties, that our lives are the equiva-*
> *lent of Hollywood stars', that we're on drugs or drinking a lot, but*
> *it's not true. Also, this is not Britain; we're not the Parliament or*
> *the elite. This is the United States, and we come from all these tiny*
> *little communities. Of course, for some people this is the big time,*
> *they come to Washington in their polyester double knits with wide*
> *eyes.*

Power and public prominence can change a man, making it very hard for a wife to keep her own equilibrium. But Roscoe feels a wife must also grow and change herself. She told us that she has come out of most of the problems in her life and marriage stronger:

> *The more prominent Ron became, the more people gravitated*
> *toward him. He received more gratification outside than inside the*
> *family. He'd be out there and audiences were cheering and women*

looking at him adoringly, and when he'd come home, I'd say, "You forgot to stop at the store for toilet paper." I never continued the hero worship when he got home. You can't.

There was this really big entertainer who had a serious crush on my husband. I found out about it because she called me up. She said, "I find your husband extremely attractive. He belongs to the people now. You have to share him."

We were doing these fund raisers in California and needed a lot of entertainers to help us out. This is how she met him. She was a singer and fell in love with him. She was very honest about it, but I was very surprised. Why would anyone that prominent find my husband so interesting? Why doesn't she go after Paul Newman or somebody else?

For a little while I was sort of flattered, but then I got panicky. I was waiting for the next thing. Was she going to say, "Well, he and I are . . . " You always hear that the wife is the last to know. At first I tried to laugh it off, but frankly it changed me considerably.

I looked at myself and thought: "I need a new hairdo, I need to dress better. I've got to read more. I wish I could sing." I started to take self-inventory, and I realized that there was a side to me that I needed to develop. I knew I was no longer going to be the same. I couldn't anymore say, "Look, I have a wedding ring, and this man isn't going anywhere."

I began to play little games with myself. How interesting. I would lose my husband to a famous entertainer. I could possibly capitalize on it. And I would get a lot of sympathy from a group of friends. But I was always thinking how I could survive it. I didn't want it to be one of these crummy breakups where they would show a picture of the handsome man and the glamorous star and this dull little wife and make it look like it was my fault.

Roscoe talked about being in the public eye and having another woman attracted to her husband. Other wives who participated in our survey told us how they felt about moving and business entertaining. They also discussed whether or not they thought life at the top was disillusioning. After looking at what they had to say, we will present some guidelines for coping with outer stresses (and in Chapter 6 we will look more closely at the "inner tensions" which accompany them).

Moving

Moving is almost always a necessary concomitant of success. The young executive must move to move up. Senior corporate officers are transferred from one office to another. Politicians, especially elected officials, move with each win, and move again with each loss. Diplomats and military personnel experience international moves. But doctors, lawyers and bankers are uprooted less often, and when they do move, it is usually within the same city and often a move "up" for the wife.

Sixty-six percent of the women we surveyed said they had moved often in order to foster their husbands' careers. These women had moved an average of eight times in their married lives, though Barbara Bush, wife of the Vice-President, told us that she has moved seventeen times, following her successful husband around the world. And MaryAnn Warner, wife of the chairman and CEO of Mobil Corporation, told us:

> *We moved six times during the first nine years of our marriage. I hated them (the moves). It was hard, lonely, and the telephone never rang. Twenty-six years later I can not let a phone go unanswered.*

In his book *Corporate Wives . . . Corporate Casualties?* psychiatrist Robert Seidenberg says that moving causes enormous trauma for executives' wives. "Wives suffer because their identities and sense of self-worth are shattered by continual moves. Unlike their husbands, for them there is neither opportunity nor energy to re-establish their importance and authority in new communities. Arduously-built credentials cannot be readily transferred again and again; after awhile one doesn't even bother. It is then that many begin to feel less than human and become ripe for tripping, tippling and tranquilization."*

*Robert Seidenberg, *Corporate Wives . . . Corporate Casualties?* (New York: American Management Association, 1980), p. vii.

A move usually means a complete change of life and sometimes a job loss for the wife. A new home, new friends, new schools, new doctors, new stores must be dealt with. So must the loss of support systems and community status. With an office waiting to receive the transferred husband, it is the wife and children who feel these losses most acutely. They are forced to build up their lives again and again.

Some women found moving much more difficult than others did. Most of the women we talked to told us that it was hardest for them to move when they were pregnant or had small children. Many said that it was hardest for children to move during the teenage years.

Polly, the wife of a highly successful insurance salesman now living in Hartford, said that moving was especially hard for her:

> *We moved four times in twelve years. One time we moved while I was six months pregnant and had a two-year-old. That time I had an anxiety attack and had to be hospitalized. I hate never being near family. I also missed sharing the new baby with old neighbors and friends.*
>
> *For me each move is worse than the last logistically, and I feel increasingly destroyed physically, intellectually, emotionally and spiritually. Although it means a career advance each time for my husband, I have to start at zero all over again. I married for roots, and I find I don't have them.*

When Polly's husband was transferred to Hartford last year, she decided to stay on temporarily in New Jersey with her children, then ten and twelve. But this decision had long-term repercussions. She told us:

> *I did not mind urging him to accept the transfer (after he had turned down many because I did not want to go) but at the same time pleading for him to go, alone. I insisted on keeping the children in school until the end of the school year, at which time I agreed to pack up and join him. He agreed to it reluctantly. It was an arrangement he was most unhappy about.*
>
> *Our son did not fare very well without his father. Our daughter and I got along fine, as basically our lives went on much as usual and we were able to finish up all our projects. Our son was tremen-*

dously happy when we finally joined Jim in Hartford, but our
daughter was devastated.

I always find it difficult to cope with adjusting myself when I
have a child who is having troubles. My first priority has to be
getting the children settled and happy and secure. Then I can start
on myself.

I arrived feeling still extremely resentful toward my husband
for having put us through another move. He was very unsympa-
thetic and said that in his view I had wrecked our marriage with
the long separation. That was definitely a low point for us. We have
not recovered from it yet, but we have enough going for us that we
are on the way up again.

Polly and Jim seemed to have mutually exclusive needs, hers for
roots and security and his for career advancement. Yet both were
committed to the marriage. Joint counseling helped them articulate
these needs and their feelings about not having them met. Once they
really "heard" each other, they stopped blaming and began rebuild-
ing. Also Jim realized that Polly and the children were important for
his sense of security, while Polly admitted that she benefited in other
ways from Jim's success at work. So their needs were not really
mutually exclusive.

With all the negative aspects of moving in mind we were surprised that almost half of our participants actually had some good
things to say about it. Beverly, one of the women we interviewed, had
started a moving consulting business as a result of her own frequent
moves. The last time her husband was transferred across the country,
she set herself up as her own transfer company, getting different
estimates, establishing a time plan, and both selling and buying their
houses. She enjoyed it so much once she approached it as a business
that she offered to help a new neighbor who was moving out soon
after Beverly and her husband moved in. Now her services are much
in demand, especially by career women who don't have the time to
spend on moving themselves.

Other women told us that they enjoyed the challenge of going
to a new location and that meeting new people was a plus. They
spoke of a forced cleaning out of old houses and old attitudes; they

welcomed change. "Dislocation often brings the family closer," said one. Even a few career women felt that moves were beneficial. A free-lance editor married to an advertising company executive told us:

> *Although I have moved a number of times during the thirty-one years of our marriage, I have had the opportunity to learn a great deal from each experience and to benefit from the ideas of many outstanding people. I have continued to pursue my own career in each new location, thereby amassing a very rich professional background.*

Shuttling between home town and husband's job location has been a solution for some political wives. Peatsy Hollings, wife of the junior Senator from South Carolina, travels between Washington and her home state twice a month. Like many other congressional couples, the Hollingses keep a home in both places.

Career women married to businessmen sometimes have commuting marriages which avoid the problems of moving but add additional strains. "I have gotten so tired of trying to maintain so many relationships in both places," lamented one such wife. "And although I clear the decks when he comes to see me, I often have to share my husband with friends and associates when I go to New York to be with him."

In an article entitled "Home Free: The Joys of Leaving Washington at Last," June Bingham (wife of the recently retired congressman from New York) looks forward to having just one home in just one city:

> *No longer do I need to commute between New York and Washington. Dearly as I love both cities, I do not love the road between them. And going by air has recently become prohibitively expensive (the government pays for members' trips, but not spouses').*
>
> *Soon I shall know where I am in the morning when I first wake up. Up to now I have had to sense whether Jonathan was on my right (New York) or on my left (Washington). As for having to commute, even in a car with 300 pages of unfinished manuscript*

and a carton of research material, surely divorces must have been granted for less frustrating cause.

> *No longer do I need to hear the pain in the voice of one of our children who has been trying for days to reach us by phone: "I didn't even know which city you were in."**

Entertaining

We asked the women we surveyed whether their husbands' jobs required an official social life, and how they felt about it. Most said yes, both giving and going to work-related parties was a very large part of their social life. Some enjoyed it. Others hated it. Some went on strike and didn't go. Others had hurt feelings if they weren't invited.

But even those who were enthusiastic about going often found it frustrating. Jennifer told us how she felt about accompanying her husband to endless social and political gatherings:

> *Are my opinions taken seriously? Absolutely not. We can meet someone and they will shake his hand and start talking to him and I am lucky if they even look in my direction. Are they going to talk, let alone listen to me? Someone will ask me, "What does your husband think about nuclear war?" and I'll say, "You have to ask him, he's over there. If you want my opinion . . . " by which time the person is already gone. I am a nonentity at these parties.*

She said that everyone assumes that she supports the same policies her husband does, so she has gradually learned to keep her opinions to herself.

> *As a result of my husband's position, and my loyalty to him, I no longer feel free to espouse any cause. This is for me the largest price to pay for being a "wife at the top."*

A doctor's wife said that she is very sociable but has a hard time mixing with people she doesn't really know:

*Washington Post, January 23, 1983.

It's hard for me to just go up to people I don't know and start up a conversation, especially when they're professional people and I don't "speak the language."

If I've had a few drinks, I can fake it and pretend to be mixing and having a good time. When I complained to Bennet about always leaving me alone at social functions, I was told that I could stay home if I wanted to. He wasn't going to change.

One Christmas he spent weeks organizing the hospital staff party. He told me that if I came, he would spend the entire evening with me because he had already put in so much time on the event. But I didn't see him the whole evening. His explanation, "Things didn't work out." And I sat all alone at the table, eight months pregnant. Everyone he knows and works with thinks he's very charming.

Harriet finds the transition from her suburban world to Steve's downtown Chicago milieu difficult. She says that she also can "fake it" but that she doesn't get anything out of joining her husband in the city for business functions. And she too doesn't like the way he behaves when they entertain officially:

Steve is a different person in that environment. He's charming, but it's like turning off and on a light. It's a different personality I see come out. Who is this person? I don't know which is the real one because at home he is very reserved.

Some women feel ill at ease with their husbands' clients or associates. Others resent having to make constant small talk and feel such events are hypocritical. A Navy captain's wife told us:

We have "all hands show" dinner parties where the commander gets up and says, "I'm so glad to see all of you here tonight" after your husband has been given a direct order to attend. That infuriates me. If they are mandatory turnouts, then they should be during work hours, in uniform, and wives shouldn't be forced to attend. Besides, I hate all the idle chatter about stupid things that goes on at these parties.

Several women pointed out that their own official entertaining was much easier when they could afford a caterer but others hated "having bartenders and waiters buzzing around the house." Most of the wives said that entertaining at home was a financial burden.

Angela gave us another perspective on official entertaining. Money was not a problem for her, but fatigue often was:

> *You get tired after a while, physically and mentally. I've had the trips, and I'm tired of it. I do what I'm expected to do, but the fun isn't there the way it used to be. But you can never let it show. You have to be gracious at all times. You never leave a receiving line unless you're going to throw up, and I've done that. I've thrown up and gone back to the receiving line.*
>
> *We're going to Alaska on business next week, and I will take along my best dresses and be polite and pleasant. Last time we were there, I felt as though I hadn't dressed quite fancily enough, even though they were in rather weird clothes themselves. I made a mistake by downplaying it too much. This time I'm going to make a big effort to say, "This is an important occasion for us. We're here, sparkling for you." Our job is to never look bored.*

But perhaps making too much of an effort, like faking it, makes official entertaining, whether at home or somewhere else, even more difficult. The wives who seemed to genuinely enjoy these functions were the ones who allowed themselves to be themselves. "It's never much fun when you are playing a part," said Maria. "I had to learn this over many years." And Jane put it this way:

> *I used to hate it but have finally learned to see the positive side of it. I used to have to be nice to certain important older people; now many people have to be nice to me. There's really some humor in this.*
>
> *I find it a responsibility to be worthy of their niceness and try to come across as interesting, non-opinionated and interested in them. When I forget about myself and get interested in them, I have more fun.*
>
> *A diplomat's wife once said that like everything in life, all this socializing has its good and bad points. Try to see the good side. If I can have just one good conversation, beyond the small-talk level, with just one person, then the evening is worth it.*

Ironically several of the former wives of successful men found that they missed the official social life after they had divorced. Joanne, the ex-wife of a high government official, said that the toughest aspect of not being part of her husband's life anymore was giving up all the social activities that went with his job. She had accepted them as part of her role, and actually as part of herself. She admitted:

> *I liked meeting people. I liked going to embassy parties. I liked to entertain. Maybe I shouldn't have been so wrapped up in it. As long as I was a part of what my former husband was doing, I enjoyed doing it because I loved him. It was also my duty and I wanted to do it. Now I feel used and exploited.*
>
> *These last few weeks there have been all these parties and luncheons for him, and I, who was steadfastly at his side for everything else, was shut out. When I told him how much it hurt me to be excluded, he said, "Nobody even noticed that you weren't there," and that made me feel even worse.*

Other Women

Roscoe Dellums talked about having other women attracted to her husband and how she handled it. Almost all the women we questioned acknowledged this problem. Their reactions varied from amusement to anxiety.

About half the women felt flattered by this kind of attention, demonstrating their own security and confidence in their husbands. They have obviously built up a level of trust as a couple. This is essentially a question of character and integrity. On the other hand, 30 percent were irritated by this outside interference and felt either annoyance or anger at their husbands' open acceptance of these attentions. And 20 percent were either unaware of their husbands' attractiveness to other women or did not care to know about it. Many attributed their husbands' popularity with other women more to their good looks, charm and intellect than to their positions.

Women who described their marriages as happy and who seemed to feel good about themselves tended to worry least about other women. The sixty-four-year-old wife of a diplomat said:

Frankly I'm more attractive than [my rivals] are. If they flirt, I joke about it and always point out to [my husband] some fault or unattractive attribute to them. I try to take care of myself so I can compete. In any event I am a very confident wife and believe he would be unlikely to find anyone to satisfy him as I do.

Another woman disagreed with Ann Landers's advice to ignore someone who is trying to get a husband's attention:

. . . I decided I wasn't going to stand around and let some tramp wreck my marriage. When she leaned over the coffee table to straighten my husband's tie (he was seated on the sofa), I gave her a swift kick in the rear and she landed in the avocado dip. It was the last time that bimbo cozied up to my George. *

Sandra, the journalist, usually steps in quickly when she senses competition:

I tell her it's a package deal. She has to take me and the kids too. I also let her know that all women love him. Once she finds out that she isn't unique, it doesn't bother me. After all, I have him.

Many women remind themselves that their husbands have chosen to stay married to them. They acknowledge that his job leads sometimes to special attention but feel that they can hold their own. A prominent politician's wife admitted to accompanying her husband to all social events and sticking by his side to discourage groupies. She wrote on her questionnaire:

Of course this happens. He is very handsome and divine. I am fortunately secure in my position and can be amused by those wretched females, usually divorced with dyed blond hair, who bat their eyes at him.

But quite a different attitude was expressed by Joanne. When she answered our questionnaire, she described her marriage as "fragile" and when we interviewed her several weeks later, her husband had moved out. She told us:

*Washington *Post*, December 7, 1982.

I thought we had a happy marriage, until one day my husband told me he no longer cared for me and that the only thing that mattered to him was his position. I tried everything I could to make his feelings change, but he had already shut me out of his life. The young women flocking around my husband made me feel very insecure. I felt he knew that he could replace me easily and it made him less likely to work on the marriage.

This is definitely part of the threat to women who are married to men in powerful positions. It takes a very committed man to turn away from it.

I fear for women who are older than I am, who never had a career and are confronted with this problem. What have they got? If a man is successful, a woman is expected to put up with a lot. "You're lucky to have this man. He is a great provider. He gives you all the security and prestige; what more do you want?"

Had my husband not been in this position, we would have worked it through, I believe. We are a casualty of the Washington scene. I paid my dues and I don't want another woman enjoying the fruits of my sacrifice. What was hardest to accept was that he did not feel any sense of obligation to me.

Joanne's husband's success went to his head. He was young and didn't handle personal power maturely. As it turned out, he gave up his wife, his home, and his child while he was in the midst of enjoying the temporary pleasures of public office. Fortunately Joanne was young and professionally qualified herself. She had a Ph.D. in nuclear physics and had written the definitive work on the effect of gamma rays on simians in space. She was able to pick up the pieces of her life and rebuild. An older woman in her situation faces a far bleaker future.

Many divorced wives of prominent men are particularly resentful if another woman ruins their marriage, and thus takes away their social status. Lorraine, the attractive ex-wife of a Midwestern banker, lived through agony when she learned of her husband's affair:

Five years ago I would have told you that I had an extremely happy marriage. But I knew of his affair for two years before I had the courage to tell him to get out. I spent an entire summer in my basement, not playing tennis, not playing golf.

I couldn't cope. It takes a lot of self-confidence to face reality.

I tell you there is not a levelheaded man in this city. I have been working part time downtown, and the advances which are made are incredible. I watch these young girls. I believe there are few men who can resist. It's an ego trip for them. You go to lunch any day of the week in any restaurant, and there is always a fifty-year-old and a kid. It's very charming for them. There is a lot of playing around. The girls are available, and they all want to get ahead. I'm not a prude. I'm a sophisticated person, but it's a different mentality.

Lorraine eventually found a job as a media consultant which opened a new area to her. She told us that she would never have been able to work as hard if she had still been married and had had to drop everything at a minute's notice to join her husband for receptions or dinners in town.

The Public Eye

It would be hard not to envy Angela. Beautiful and gracious, she goes out of her way to put everyone at ease. But during a lengthy interview in her elegant penthouse she talked about some of the stresses of her life. They had definitely left their mark on her health and psyche. She told us:

I am a chronic worrier, and at times my grinding worry over my husband's health and safety nearly puts me away. He has been plagued by the usual groups, so we have to go underground as have so many other public figures. The security measures are always with us and to a lesser degree with our children.

She told us what it feels like to be constantly in the public eye:

Neither of us likes it, but my husband handles it better than I do. What hurts most is when the media criticism is based on sloppy and incomplete investigation and its biases show.

Newspaper people have always been wrong about my husband.

They have allowed themselves to be used by those who have not wished him well. It's almost impossible to get a fair hearing under such circumstances, which is infuriating. One is so helpless.

We asked others of our participants how they felt about being in the public eye and how they handled media criticism. The majority of the women we surveyed had been written about in the newspaper, and roughly one third of them were considered constantly "newsworthy" by the media. Most of them didn't like being monitored. However, many accepted it as a necessary evil. Musha Brzezinski said:

I knew the situation was temporary. I got irritated at first, and then got used to it. I realized that the critics were basically hypocritical.

For political wives life in Washington seemed to be difficult and sometimes dangerous, although it was fascinating. Many a wife who had expressed her opinion frankly on an issue found that she was quoted in one of the next day's papers. Eileen, the Senator's wife, told us:

I know enough not to talk to Sally Quinn [a gossip columnist for the Washington Post], but even in our home state we have to be careful. There you know your next door neighbor is reading the same paper.

A congressman whose bill is being debated in the House needs the publicity the media provide; his wife, on the other hand, has to watch her appearance, her language and even her driveway. The Senator's wife still gets angry remembering her latest run-in with the press:

It was seven in the morning, and I had just poured my husband a cup of coffee when a TV crew pulled up in front of our house. They were hoping he would comment on an issue that he was very involved in at that moment.

I can't articulate anger very well, but I told them, "Next time you are planning an attack, please call ahead . . ."

Jean Sisco learned through the experience of others to be careful. She prefers a less visible life-style:

We've never been part of the beautiful-people set. We opted for us. I gather from some wives that they bitterly resent being used, but I've never felt that. I've gone to some parties that I'd rather not attend, but we've never felt it was necessary to have a lot of social press.

I have one small overriding fear. I have seen what has happened in Washington to people who become adored by the press, how quickly they were dropped by the press. I have never wanted to stick my neck out that far.

Unfortunately not all political wives have that option. Once a man makes policy, he's fair game for the press, often to the horror of his family. Another Washington wife said:

My instinct is to kill! I don't trust the press; although I love it when it's a good article.

Dottie Blackmun feels quite differently about her own association with the press.

I have never gotten into any jams with the press. If they ask me something that's not appropriate, I say, "Well, I guess I shouldn't discuss that."

Generally I like the news people. They never feel that I'm trying to hide or shade something. Once they find out you're honest, they're for you. If they think you're fudging it and lying, then they don't like it very much. I understand that they have a job to do and need to be aggressive in gathering the news. I don't like it when a reporter or columnist attacks my husband unfairly on a subject about which the columnist isn't fully informed of the facts or on which he has a biased opinion. Usually I become angry and upset, and want to call or write him, but after a few days am able to laugh about it.

Revelations about their private lives, be it on the front page, on the editorial page or in the gossip columns, is definitely a mixed blessing for the wives who have experienced it. We found that wives feel criticism perhaps more strongly than their husbands do, but they also enjoy the recognition it brings. Jennifer told us:

> *I do not enjoy criticism. Who does? But I suffer much more than my husband does even though it's mostly directed against him. My skin is thicker today than it was ten years ago, but it still hurts.*
>
> *On the other hand, I love praise while in the public eye, and you can't have one without the other.*

Illusions and Disillusions

In answering the question "Is life at the top disillusioning?" most women said that it depended on what illusions you had before you arrived. Those who felt it was disillusioning cited different reasons for their feelings. Joanne found the deepest disillusionment not with others at the top but with her husband when he got there. She told us unhappily:

> *Power and prestige weakened his character, and that was definitely disillusioning. Values become distorted. What used to be important to him before, family, sharing time, sharing himself, was just thrown out the window. Success and power became his primary goal. The one at the top has to cancel his humanity.*
>
> *Once the priceless poverty of struggling to get there is over, each partner goes his or her own way. The illusions of a perfect marriage vanish in the cold light of success and all that it entails.*

Finding out that her husband had changed and that they no longer shared common values was extremely painful for Joanne. She realized that she also had become "sucked into" an unreal society living in a unreal world. When she was separated from that world, much of her identity and sense of self-worth seemed to have been left behind with her husband. But gradually, as she re-examined her marriage and her husband's success, she concluded that she was well out of it. "It's not worth the loneliness and frustration," she said.

Other women told us that their primary disillusionment came from finding out that others at the top have feet of clay, that men at the top sometimes maintain their positions there by politicking and backstabbing, and that critical decisions are often made on irrelevant grounds. They discovered that on closer inspection some people in top positions are not really competent to be there. Angela told us:

> *It looks extremely glamorous to others, and to a degree it is, but it wears off fast. I always had the impression that life got easier as you neared your goals, but everything seems to get more compli-cated. You find that you have to struggle to stay at the top just as you had to struggle to get there.*
>
> *Wealth, power and position really do not provide happiness and fulfillment. Those who expect them to are going to be disillusioned. It's only material gilt, and that is not where the joys of life are.*

Nearly one quarter of our participants said that life at the top wasn't disillusioning because they had no illusions about it in the first place. They felt that they had known all along what it would be like and were perhaps even too cynical. "I had no illusions, so I had none to lose," said one. "Life, whether at the top or elsewhere, is hard, often boring, and too short."

Another group frankly loved sharing their husbands' prestige and the benefits of their success. "Having enough money to pay the bills is definitely not disillusioning," said the wife of a TV newscaster. "I can't imagine how it could be disillusioning if a man strives for success, achieves it, and his wife basks in his reflected glory." Many of these women found it exciting and rewarding to join their hus-bands in the limelight. "Who else gets to dine with royalty and visit Princess Grace?" the wife of a politician asked us. She thought the question about disillusionment was "stupid!" "Who says so? Nancy Kissinger? Or Rosalind Carter? Probably someone who has never been there. Of course not!"

However, the most thoughtful answers to this question came from women who seemed realistic about the difficulties and dangers of life at the top as well as appreciative of its rewards. Carol told us:

> *It can be exciting and meaningful, and I feel very fortunate for all the opportunities I've had. But life, at the top or the bottom,*

is what you make of it. If you're there to do something rather than to be something, you won't be disillusioned.

Wealth can be enjoyed without squandering it. The more time spent doing for others, the less time one has to worry about oneself. Also, work never hurt anyone. We are often too eager to hire someone to do for us.

To paraphrase Emerson: "To have beauty, you must carry it with you."

Summing Up

Wives of very successful men suffer from some very unique stresses, such as official entertaining and being in the public eye. They also often cope with frequent moves and the interest of other women in their husbands. The stresses sometimes lead to burnout, but they can also be dealt with constructively.

Guidelines

1. Remember Roscoe Dellums's admonition: "A wife must also grow and change herself."
2. Moving is never easy, but try to see it as an opportunity to clean out old attitudes as well as the old house.
3. Try to make the move with your husband. Don't let him saddle you with all the responsibilities, but don't force him to go alone. Talk to each other. If your needs are different, try to work out a mutually acceptable solution.
4. If you have a hard time at your husband's office parties, try to have a good talk with just one person and the evening will be worthwhile. Remember, everyone else is probably feeling as ill at ease as you are.
5. If you're not invited to an official function, don't take it personally. If you are, don't let it go to your head.
6. Build trust with your husband by working on your marriage.
7. Be frank with the media, but don't become seduced by them.
8. Try not to become cynical about life at the top. Remember, to have beauty you must carry it with you.

6

INNER TENSIONS

Mildred

"I am a *nothing,* a nonperson" was Mildred's answer to the question "If someone asked you who *you* were, what would you answer?" Mildred was the wife of a businessman and civic leader of a large Southern city. Not long before we interviewed her, she had walked out of her family home and filed for divorce after fifty-one years of marriage. Now seventy-five, she was eager to talk about her experiences. "I hope that something I have said might help a younger wife in a similar position," Mildred told us.

Mildred's husband, Joel, did not have the visible success of a politician or statesman. He did not move in the moneyed circles of Fortune 500 companies. But Mildred experienced the stresses of his work and life-style just as much as the wife of a more obviously successful man. Of all the women we surveyed she suffered most from the tensions caused by the outer stresses discussed in the last chapter.

Joel owned his own company and was extremely successful financially. Joel and Mildred lived in a large house and were able to afford to send their children to the best Ivy League colleges. But as Mildred told us, Joel had too many concerns of his own to be interested in her. Whatever time he had left over after his workday he spent on community affairs. Whatever money they had left over after paying their personal bills he spent on community improvements. Mildred felt that their marriage began to crumble after what should have been one of its finest moments, a testimonial dinner held to honor Joel:

We had a happy marriage for thirty-seven years. There were problems of course, but none so serious as to call for separation or divorce. One problem was my growing unhappiness at being taken for granted. Undoubtedly I'm at fault for encouraging my husband in his community participation because in time that, and his work, became his complete life with no time for me. He was successful in everything he did, he refused to fail in anything. He did so much for our town that the local business association had a testimonial dinner on his behalf. Over three hundred guests paid out good money and gave up an evening to hear him being praised! For the next fourteen years of our marriage things got worse and worse. I'm certain now that he was affected by the praise he had received at that testimonial dinner. It turned his head.

Mildred said that because her husband was completely caught up in his outside activities, they never did anything together as a couple. Even before the testimonial dinner Joel had been the dominant partner in the marriage; after it he became more and more overpowering. Mildred continued:

There were fourteen unhappy years of marriage for me before I walked out on my husband. During those years there were changes in my husband's personality. He was increasingly aggressive: a no-nonsense person who put all his energy into his work and the community challenges that came his way. I never envied my husband's success, only deplored his lack of time for me.

I know that my health was affected by his personality as the years went on. He was a perfectionist, and I found it impossible to live according to his rules instead of mine. For example, we often had to entertain business guests at home. At first it was fun, but not when my husband began to criticize me. The food wasn't prepared as he wished (meat overdone or underdone, etc.), and he often criticized my responses to our guests. I hated the post mortems! I developed fibrillation of my heart and high blood pressure as a result of the tensions.

Joel did not treat me as a person. He took me for granted. He said he loved me, but it was obvious from his lack of attention to me that he did not know what love was. I stopped loving him and was unhappy with sex, which he demanded on the spot, in the early evening, long before I was ready to retire, or at 2 A.M., when he would awaken me from sleep. In other words, when he was ready, he wanted sex. I resented that because when I wanted something from him, he had no time for me.

Over the years our marriage became less and less normal. My husband was not good at small talk, but he never had anything to say to me. He always had a lot on his mind, and he did not like to be interrupted in his thoughts except for important matters. Nothing I said was important to him, so I learned not to speak unless I was spoken to.

We used to drive to Michigan for our vacation every summer. I recall one eighteen-hour drive when scarcely a word was spoken in the car. I hated that. At home there were weeks at a time when he said not one word to me. We passed each other in the room like strangers. Who needs to live that way?

I can't explain what has happened to my husband over the years except that he has been corrupted by money and power. He does not understand human values.

Mildred admitted that many of her problems came more from Joel's personality than from his work per se; but it seemed to have been his work and his success at it that reinforced the negative aspects of his personality. We would link her inner tensions (her health and sex problems as well as her feeling of being a "nonperson") to her husband's success as well. Not all men let success go to their heads, as many of our participants told us. And husbands and wives are often able to keep communication going in spite of work and other demands. But some men, like Joel, who get tremendous positive reinforcement outside the home, seem unable to function well within it. Other women told us that they too had health problems attributable to the pressures of their husbands' success, and many spoke of a poor sex life. And some, particularly those with unfulfilling marriages, identified with Mildred's description of herself as a "nothing."

Who Are You?

Louise, whom we quoted in Chapter 4, when asked who she would say *she* was, answered, "I fear I'm his wife," echoing 26 percent of the women we talked to. Louise admitted her marriage was shaky and added, "I'd probably say Mrs. So and So with no future. I don't feel I have developed my own potential because my husband overshadows me." A doctor's wife told us sadly:

> *I don't know who I am. I am really disappointed, miserable and saddened by what my life has become. I nearly killed myself attaining things and helping others. Now I am nowhere.*

Only after getting professional counseling did Phyllis change her self-image. She wrote on her questionnaire:

> *I am trying to view myself as a responsible adult instead of a passive person with low self-esteem. Until a few months ago I was nobody, with no redeeming features. I felt I was the root of all my problems. Now I have begun to see myself as a valuable human being. The change feels so good!*

However, Mildred defined herself as a "nothing" one year after she finally left Joel. Deciding on divorce and finally carrying it out left Mildred free but mentally drained. She too needed professional help to put her psyche and identity back together, but at the time we interviewed her, she was neither seeking nor getting this kind of help. Her grown children remained her strongest supports. Her age and her fear of letting others in her community know of her problems kept her from developing a more extensive support system.

Many of the women we talked to who listed "his wife" first when asked who *they* were, seemed fulfilled by the role. Here are some of their comments:

> *I am a very capable corporate wife, a good mother and a reasonably interesting person.*

> *My husband's wife, my children's mother and a stained-glass artist, in that order. I have worked hard at my identity, and feel more comfortable with myself than ever before.*

*I'm a disappearing breed, a housewife, an enriched, enlight-
ened, creative person, but still a housewife, and I like it. I feel these
are two very important roles and necessary for a smoothly running
household. It's because I do my job well that my husband is able
to do what he does.*

We were reminded here of Evans and Bartolome's distinction
between martyrs and choosers. Those women who had never worked
out their own identity within their marriage were called martyrs.
Those who had come to terms with themselves, no matter what they
had decided to be or do, were called choosers. Obviously the women
quoted above are choosers, which is why they are happy in the role
of housewife.

When asked what they would answer if asked who they were, 30
percent of our participants said, "Give my own name." Other answers given were mother, friend, neighbor, member of organization
and career woman. In fact 11 percent defined themselves primarily
through their careers. These were typical responses:

*My career has been a joy, and doing some mind dialing over
the various roles I play, I would say, librarian.*

*No problem. It would be me plus what I do. Writer. But I'd
be very conscious of the years of floundering with that question
before I could give that answer.*

*Chairman of a nonprofit organization in education. In some
cases I would mention other interests, such as music.*

Others interpreted the question on a deeper level. These were two
of the most interesting answers:

*Most people know who I am, since, as a New Yorker, I like to
make instant and existential contact. Tell me not about your
parents and children but what you think of life's meaning.*

*I am a child of God, first of all. I feel that I am a pilgrim on
a journey. "Happy is the man or woman who finds wisdom, and
the man or woman who gets understanding. For the gain from it
is better than gain from silver and its profit better than gold."
(Proverbs 3:13)*

And finally, here is Barbara Bush's sensitive answer to this question:

The world's most fortunate woman, who, I hope, helps others.

What Would You Do If He Left You Tomorrow?

When we began to write this book, we had certain preconceived ideas about the way we wanted it to turn out. We were not just asking the women who participated in our survey to tell us about their problems; we were also intent on discovering their ways of coping with these problems. We wanted our book to have a happy ending, so we structured the questionnaire and the interviews based upon it to end with the good news; it can be done, you can be happy, here are some guidelines that have helped others.

In the course of our research we stumbled on something which made us feel that we were on the right track and which made sense of our other perceptions. This discovery came when we connected the answers to the question "What would you do if he left you tomorrow?" with the answers to "How do you rate your marriage now?" The majority of women who rated their marriages as good to excellent were able to see themselves functioning independently if their husbands left. They were not happy about the idea, but typical replies were: "Continue to work, continue to dance." "I would take charge of my life and make sure my son was well provided for." "My husband's success has taught me independence."

It seems evident that a strong marriage breeds an independent, self-confident wife. Or perhaps an independent wife who can imagine herself coping and developing on her own builds a stronger marriage. Or both.

The opposite also appears to be true. Wives who were unhappy about their marriages, who wrote "poor" or "miserable" when rating them on the first page of the questionnaire and then told us about their unhappiness for the next five pages, often wrote "Fall apart" or "Commit suicide" when asked what they would do if their husbands left tomorrow. We were amazed at this. Escape from an unhappy and demeaning marriage looked like life rather than death to us. We wanted to write these women back and say "Get out!" but weren't able to because of the anonymity of their replies. Though we are not often advocates of divorce, we found that there were some women who were living in their own private hell. And there they stayed, until (as often happened in these cases) their husbands finally did leave.

The following quote is from an interview with Michelle, the diplomat's ex-wife:

> *I was the old-fashioned type, doing everything for him. Never thought about myself at all. Everything was directed towards his career, his needs, my children's needs. I was trying to be as perfect as I could in every possible way. I did everything I could for his career, and for the State Department. He took it for granted. He didn't think it was extraordinary. It was the way I was, and he had been used to it. I was useful to Greg. He was a very calculating person, but that I didn't see.*
>
> *Greg was intelligent and very manipulating. He knew how to handle the reinforcement and the fear by punishing the children or me when he thought we were straying from the right path. He managed to keep me under complete control and fear. My mother kept asking me, "Why do you fear him so?" I was afraid of him because I was afraid that I could not meet his expectations. I was very much a little girl who wants to please.*

Greg walked out on Michelle after eighteen years of marriage, saying he wanted to marry his latest mistress. Even though she had been miserable in her marriage, Michelle couldn't imagine herself functioning without him. "Identity!" she exclaimed. "That went out the window when I took my marriage vows."

> *I never thought of leaving him because I always hoped things might get better. Looking back, I realize that I had stayed very childish. I couldn't face reality and didn't even want to.*

Forced to face reality, Michelle contemplated suicide. It was her two sons who kept her alive through this period. But eventually Michelle enrolled in college and started working toward a career. "Changing and growing hurts," she said, "but not to grow is to die.

I realize that now. Who wants to be a fifty-year-old little girl? It's really a grotesque image, isn't it?"

Audrey's life experience was very different from Michelle's. She is a good example of a happily married woman with a strong sense of her own identity. She is a psychologist, her husband a prominent attorney. She is also the mother of seven children:

> *We are both very independent people. What amuses us is that all of my husband's friends think that he is henpecked and all of my friends think he bosses me around. That's an interesting commentary on the relationship and on the perception of other people on our marriage.*

> *When our oldest child started high school, I realized that the family had been an absorption of mine and I enjoyed it tremendously. But the children had to leave too, and they would probably leave the nest in much the way their father had, with great ease and pleasure. And therefore, I needed something to fill these hours. That was a very good decision, and very well supported by my husband.*

> *Also I wanted to be paid for my work. I wanted an income of my own, which everyone thought was very funny. The first year I made two thousand dollars, and John's partners joked, "Oh, now John can retire."*

> *I can't expect John to find me interesting if I don't find myself interesting. I can't take an interest in his work if I'm not doing something interesting myself. We got to the point where we were financially comfortable, emotionally in good shape, the kids were fine, and now what was I going to do for the next fifty years? I certainly wasn't going to hang around waiting to go to a convention once a year, or a dinner party now and then. I needed something that made me feel worthwhile and productive, as if I were making a contribution too.*

Audrey told us that if John left her, she would try to get a good financial settlement, continue raising the kids and practicing her profession, and "toward late evening, I would probably have a good cry."

Do You Envy Him?

For some women we questioned it was difficult not to envy their husband and his success. Joanne said:

> *I see him bask in all the glory publicly and never acknowledge privately how much I've contributed to it. He has the money and the power to come and go pretty much as he pleases. I would love half the attention he gets. He loves his job, is good at what he does and is constantly having his ego massaged.*

In most cases it was women with poor marriages who envied their husbands the most, although many happily married women admitted to having gone through a stage of envying their husbands in the past. Roscoe Dellums wrote:

> *I have been envious in the past about my husband's success, and now that I'm beginning anew as a lawyer, I wish I were as young as he was when he got started. Of course, envying Ron was more of a problem before I had my own professional objectives clarified. Now that I'm realizing my own opportunities, I no longer envy his success. I am, however, realistic about the age, sex and race discrimination I may be confronted with. Also, I do envy the salary he is able to command.*
>
> *But I've also seen close up the incredible responsibility that goes with his position. In the past I've been asked to substitute for Ron when he had a speaking engagement. Pleasing the public is a very difficult task.*

Jane told us that she had envied her husband earlier in her life when she was marking time in a dull job. But now, between mothering and studying Chinese, she has all the emotional and intellectual stimuli she could ask for. She said that she had been jealous not so much of his success as of the meaning that his work had for him. "I wanted *full days* doing things I cared about as much as he cared about his work," she said.

Some women admitted to envying their successful husbands for their life-styles. Shirley, the wife of a top government official, wrote:

He drives around in a limousine, and I don't even have help in the house. And I'm always stuck at home while he travels around the world. It's hard not to envy him then. Sometimes I wish that I had the luxury of travel that he does. However, I was disappointed when I did accompany him on a working trip. It was all work!

Others told us that they envied their husbands something less tangible but even more important, their singleness of vision and the luxury of pursuing it. "His tunnel vision" is the way one woman described it:

He seems to have so few choices and doesn't get all mixed up emotionally the way I do. He is totally committed to one thing. That's what I envy, his single-mindedness. Next to him I feel like a butterfly.

But more than half of the women in our survey said that they didn't envy their husbands. They felt that their husbands' success was more than deserved, and they were proud of their part in its achievement. They were also glad that the pressure was on their husbands and not on them. Many took tremendous satisfaction in their husbands' success. Dottie Blackmun was one of these:

I don't envy him. He is a very self-effacing person. I don't know anyone who deserves it more!

Carol, the executive's wife, agreed:

His success delights me. He has worked very hard for it, never stepped on others to achieve it, and it's right for him. I am thrilled by what he has achieved. Occasionally I've been a bit uncomfortable about the unearned benefits that I've gained just by being his wife. Mostly, I've enjoyed it. Sometimes I've wished that I were more successful, but I've never wished him less successful.

Is He Ever Jealous of You?

We turned the tables and asked whether these women thought their husbands were ever jealous of them. Carol said that her husband got vicarious pleasure from her artistic pursuits but that she didn't think that he envied her for them. But 32 percent of our participants answered this question yes. What were their husbands jealous of? What did they envy? The answers are interesting.

There were three frequently given reasons for husbands envying wives. The majority of women who answered this question affirmatively told us that their husbands were envious of their relationship with the children. Typical of these women, Louise wrote:

> *I think that he is jealous of my ability to relate to the children, and to read them like books. He would deny this. Women overeat and men deny. I have a relationship with the children that he doesn't have. I enjoy the children and am close to them. He isn't. If he goes in to help them dress in the morning, they say, "No, we want Mommy."*

The second most common thing that these women said their husbands envied was their ease with people and their ability to express their feelings. Hard-driving, perfectionist men envied their wives' more easygoing personalities and expressiveness. "I know he enjoys my freer spirit and my stronger ability to express emotions because he would like to be more like that himself," said Carol.

Third, some wives said that they thought their husbands envied their free time and flexible time, and the variety of their activities. "Sometimes I think he would really just like to go back to bed after breakfast," wrote Angela. "But of course he can't. Once you're on the fast track, it's hard to get off without crashing."

What Others Think

The prominence and visibility of successful men and their wives, whether they are at the top of the small-town pyramid or national figures, often makes them concerned about what others will think. Everybody worries about this to some extent, but the women we talked to told us that this was an ongoing problem for them. "If there is a company social occasion and I don't have the *perfect* thing to wear, I'd rather not go," said the wife of the president of a manufacturing firm. "I'm overly concerned. I make a big effort to keep my weight down and never go out of the house without looking my best, even to the grocery store. I wish I didn't feel I had to."

Everyone seems to have ideas about what these women should look like and how they should behave. Every new first lady is greeted with a running commentary in the press. If she is well dressed and well coiffed, she is accused of being superficial. If she is interested in politics, people say that she is making herself an unofficial member of the Cabinet. If she isn't interested in politics, she is considered a lightweight. She's damned if she does and damned if she doesn't.

Effi Barry is the wife of the mayor of Washington, D.C. In a column in the Washington *Post*, Dorothy Gilliam quoted a close friend as saying of Effi, "She is imprisoned in other people's illusions and expectations." The article proceeded to sympathize with Effi's need for more privacy and anonymity for family and health reasons and then concluded:

> . . . there is an important role that Effi Barry could play now, an extension of one she has already played. She has made many appearances in local schools, telling young people, she says, "to get out of their neighborhoods, benefit from the magnificence of this city." . . . They need more than just to be told to grow, to gain self-confidence or to feel part of the whole city. They need concrete help to accomplish those things, and Effi Barry could be in a unique position to give it.*

One can't help feeling that if Effi is concerned with what others think of her, she will once more muster her inner forces and do the right and noble thing for the city of Washington. But what about doing the right thing for Effi Barry?

Outside of the nation's capital, in the smaller cities and towns of America, there are millions of women who are just as pressured as Effi Barry because their husbands too are successful. These are the words of the wife of a bank president in Oklahoma:

> *I am overly concerned, I guess. I have to watch what I say, which is hard for me. I don't like criticism and don't take it very well. We're very visible around here.*
>
> *My appearance is always watched. What I have to say would*

*February 7, 1983.

be repeated, so I'm very careful. I take it for granted and will do anything to promote Henry's career.

Must a wife sacrifice her autonomy for her husband's career? Some women do, and all wives must to some extent. Much depends on how their husbands feel about it. Maria, the ambassador's wife who talked about the problems she experienced in making friends, said that her husband's attitude toward the "what will other people think" problem really helped her. In Maria's words:

> *We were much younger than our predecessors, and when we arrived at our overseas posts, I found a lot of duties and memberships just waiting to fall on my shoulders. Some of these were important and part of the team effort my husband and I believed in. But some of them were silly; something that had occupied the ambassador's wife before me because she didn't have young children (which I did) and had a lot of time on her hands.*
>
> *I remember one horrible club I joined that really did nothing; as far as I could see, they met together every now and then and did nothing. I came home very depressed from the third meeting of this group and told my husband how dead everyone seemed there. "Then you better get out of it, or you'll end up as dead as they are," my husband said.*
>
> *I quit and lightning didn't strike me.*

But other men seemed highly concerned about what their wives did or said. They were very conscious of their wives' public behavior and did not want them ever to indicate that they might not be perfect wives. But who likes perfect people? Nobody, because they don't seem real. And they make others feel less than perfect by comparison. Men who pressure their wives this way are often insecure about their own imperfections.

Sex

To introduce our discussion of sex and the successful man, we would like to quote a long letter from a woman we will call Gail. Gail was not one of the original participants in our survey. She saw us on a television program about *Coping with His Success* and wrote us immediately. "I couldn't take my eyes off the screen," Gail said. "You were talking about me!"

You might find my situation enlightening. I am the second wife of an over-achieving "man at the top."

I was thirty-one years old and in an unfulfilling but not horrible marriage. I managed the children. He managed the job. We grew apart. He thought we were happy. I knew that I was not. There just had to be more. Every woman's magazine or Donahue show I saw told me that I was justified to expect more. I was entitled.

Money was not in abundance in this marriage, but we had the usual trappings. Money was not what I missed. I missed the closeness. That new thing everyone was talking about, "meaningful communication." To be seen as a separate worthwhile person. It all made sense to me.

Oh, how we were all influenced by the changes of womanhood in the seventies. Everywhere we turned we were bombarded. The media, leaders of women's groups, everyone. We were told, "Wake up, American women. You have choices!" CHOICES??? What an ambiguous word. Choices to what? Go braless, have affairs, demand our rights, have an orgasm, get a job, run away from home? Wow, it boggled the mind.

One segment of Madison Avenue told us we weren't getting older, we were getting better. While the only image they used to sell us their products was a peaches and cream, wrinkleless, stretch-markless, skinny eighteen-year-old model. If that did not add to our confusion, more and more of our friends' husbands were bailing out for other women. Mostly younger women. Much younger.

I was in a daze. I did what millions of American women did. I reacted to it, all of it. In my own upper-middle-class way I did what all the magazines and talk shows told me millions of American women were doing. I had an affair. I didn't just have an affair. I decided to have an affair and looked for a prospect.

I had all the qualifications. I was unhappy. Something was missing. I had just passed thirty, and I was scared to death that I would wake up in twenty years and find out that I would still be in the same spot. Still unhappy and still lonely. Too old to have choices. It would be too late. Who would want me then? I couldn't bear the thought of never being in love again.

My affair was with another Mr. Man at the Top. You need to know that I didn't seduce this man. I didn't have to. It was so easy. He was on the move, all I had to do was be attentive and responsive when the calls started. He didn't have time for his wife and children, his law practice was very demanding. But he did have time for me.

We went on picnics in the middle of the day. We bought each other fun, wonderful gifts. We drank wine in his car as we were awed by the beautiful fall leaves in the woods. We bundled up in jackets and gloves and met for long silent walks in snow-covered parks. We went to romantic out-of-the-way restaurants and had dinner by candlelight.

Soon every minute we were apart was torture. We finally leased an apartment in a wonderful old house in the campy college section of our town. It was so fantastic. We were so in love. We couldn't take our eyes off each other, much less our hands. I felt like I was living in a dream. We made love at a pitch that I had never known existed. He said that he felt alive for the first time in years. He claimed his wife only cared about the designer dresses, winter vacations and all the money he made. He was in love with me. It was a dream. It was wonderful.

It was also wrong. Everything about it told me it was wrong. I could not handle the feeling of being the other woman. It was hard to fight off the cheapness of it. The guilt of telling lies and seeing the look of hurt on my husband's face.

I could not help but wonder if he gave his wife as much love and attention as he gave me. I wondered how much of their trouble was his fault. If he had his career and me, how much could he give her? I finally, after a million tears, got the courage to break it off and mean it. I realize now that I hoped he would leave his wife, that he would see he could not live without me. He said he was crushed. His life was over. He took his wife on a trip to Sweden and by now, I am sure, has moved on to another affair. Life goes on.

I was never the same. I had experienced what all the women's magazines and talk shows had been telling me was out there. There was no way I could ever go back. An affair was not a viable alternative for me. I could not handle it. But I could not handle the prospect of living the way I had been living forever. I now knew it was not all over. I now knew that someone could still love me. I was still a desirable person. There could still be fireworks. I did have choices.

I got a job. My first in eleven years. It was an adjustment but also wonderful. People related to me, and not just as Lisa, Jenny and Peter's mom. ME! I worried about leaving my children with a sitter. I didn't see much of them. But someone said, "It's quality time, not quantity time that counts," so I was ok. I filed for divorce.

It was not long before another Mr. Man at the Top, who worked at the same company, began to make passes. I was so neat and attractive . . . professional, bright and alive, he said. His wife only cared about the children. She stayed in her bathrobe. Never made a decent dinner, or cleaned the house. She was always depressed and had gotten fat. She was boring. He was miserable, he claimed. How much he admired me for taking the risk to get out of a bad marriage. I was an inspiration to him. He filed for divorce.

Our courtship was a dream. He treated me like a queen. The attention, the silly things, the sex, the communication, it was fantastic. Everything I had heard was right. It was possible to have it all. You just had to take the risk.

We dated for two years while he and his wife fought in court over the property. He said she was a crazy slob. I believed him.

We wanted to be sure that we didn't make the same mistakes that we had made the first time. We wanted to be sure we had all the answers. We would always be able to protect our relationship. We were the risk-takers of the late seventies. Other couples looked at us with envy.

We saw a counselor for six months before we married. During that period my Man at the Top claimed he could see that a lot of the problems in his first marriage had been his fault. He had never worked on their relationship. He had devoted all his time and energy to his job. Put his priorities in the wrong places. He could see that to keep what we had, he could not make those mistakes again. He was committed to always putting US first and his job second.

The wedding was wonderful. Our closest friends, my three children, his two. We left for a month's honeymoon in Europe. When we didn't wear each other out talking, we wore each other out in bed. I never dreamed life could be so wonderful. Thank God for all those women and writers who said, "There's more." "You don't have to settle." "Go for it."

As we sat on the plane on the way back to the States from our honeymoon, my new husband said, "Now that the wedding is over, our life can get back to normal." GET BACK TO NORMAL! What did he mean? I was soon to find out.

If he made love to me more than once a month, I had to seduce him. Then it was less than exciting. He brought home work, and when he didn't, he was mentally a thousand miles away or he fell asleep in front of the TV.

He didn't have time for romantic lunch-time picnics. He had clients to entertain. What was my problem? Didn't I understand? He had a career. When I tried to talk to him, remind him he was doing the same thing that smothered his first marriage, that I felt lonely and missed what we had had before, he was less than kind. He said, "I can't do my job and pay attention to you too. I lost a lot of ground with my career when I was putting so much energy into our relationship. I have a lot to make up for. Good grief, find something to keep yourself busy. Go to the club. Play bridge, do something, and get off my back!"

To say that I was in a state of shock would be an understatement. I felt like I had been hit by a truck. So this was marriage to the Man at the Top. No wonder his wife got fat and was too depressed to get dressed.

The first three years of our marriage were like a bad dream. I went from periods of such acute depression that I had to take drugs just to get through the days, to trying to be the best-looking, most wonderful wife that ever existed, constantly striving for his attention and approval. Nothing worked.

In all the thought and panic that I have been through these last four years I have come to the conclusion that maybe it doesn't get any better than this. If you are a bright, achieving woman, you want a bright, achieving man. A weak man with no ambition will never make you happy. But how do you fight the loneliness when you get to the top and find that there is no one there to share it with?

For myself, I am doing the only thing I know to do. Trying to be the best I can be. I must be good, look good, entertain well but as someone once said, I am dancing as fast as I can.

Among my peers I see a lot of desperate women. Some are fat and frumpy. Some drink. Some pop Valium or worse. Some sleep around. Some leave. Some seem to be on the edge of a cliff. On the brink of disaster. This is not just the simple problem of keeping a spoiled, rich wife happy. I see this as a serious problem.

As we run to the therapists that our husbands can well afford, we find out that it is a mistake to ever look to another person for your happiness and self-worth. Does it make any more sense to fill all the empty time with some well-meaning project just to stay alive, interesting and sane? You work hard to keep him, you work hard to keep your self-respect, and you work hard to stay in your right mind. And all the time you wonder if it is all worth it.

In her letter Gail touches on many points that our participants made concerning sex and the successful man. She also makes an interesting commentary on the rising expectations of women in the seventies and eighties. Do Gail and other women like her really have the choices that magazines and talk shows trumpet? What are these choices now that doctors and *National Geographic* photographers have proved that going braless leads not to liberation but to sagging breasts? Is there hope for Gail in her second marriage to a man at the top? We think that she already has the solution to her problems, but before we answer these questions, we want to discuss the subject of sex at the top in general.

Approximately one third of our participants said that the pressures of their husbands' jobs had not had a negative effect on their sex lives. Audrey told us: "We find that sex gets better and better. We're very close and have always found sex to be consummate communication."

"Our sex life improves when he's feeling successful and self-confident. Sex is an outlet for him; he seems to need it more when he is stressed," said the wife of a Madison Avenue executive.

However, the majority (67 percent) of the women we surveyed told us that long hours, frequent travel, and job-related stress had affected their sex lives with their husbands. Some wives also said that their husbands' attitudes toward sex, typically more performance-oriented than romantic, often left them less than satisfied. But many accepted a mediocre sex life as a trade-off for marriage to a successful man. Most rated their marriages as good to excellent. In a study entitled *Sex and the Significant Americans*,* sociologists John Cuber and Peggy Harroff found that what they called the instrumental marriage was prevalent among successful people. In the instrumental marriage an unspoken arrangement has been arrived at by husband and wife that he is the source of income and status but has only a minimal time and emotional commitment to the family. For her part the wife assumes the duties of taking care of the house and children and is free to spend the rest of her time as she pleases. Both marriage partners see the marriage as happy, though neither describes it as vital or dynamic.

Executive and official travel plays havoc with a regular, normal sex life. Of course it is difficult to make love with someone who is in Japan when you're in Chicago. One woman with a traveling husband told us:

> *You feel like a whore at times. If he leaves on Sunday, then Saturday night is packing and making love, just part of the schedule. If you don't do it, then nothing for who knows how long. There is absolutely no spontaneity. It's great for birth control. When I was trying to get pregnant, he was always away.*

*Baltimore, Md.: Penguin Books, 1966.

Others maintained that a demanding work schedule often left their husbands too tired for sex even when they weren't traveling. Many men were so exhausted that they simply collapsed after a hard day at work. Others were too preoccupied to be interested. Still others seemed either to have a naturally low sex drive or to have diverted their sexual energy into professional achievement. Perhaps many took an almost sexual satisfaction in their power and position. Some seemed to get more real gratification from the adulation of their employees, constituents or clients than from making love to their wives. The wife of a nationally known scientist contended:

> Most of these high achievers are not highly motivated sexually. It's just that they picture themselves as such. With that kind of high intellectual achievement, they also think of themselves as being very sexy. But they're not. At least my husband isn't.

Other women told us that it was their husbands' attitudes toward sex that bothered them the most. They felt that their husbands rushed through sex as one more thing to be accomplished and cleared out of the way. The little touches and, even more important, the emotional connections were missing. The following quote is from Jennifer, the young congressman's wife:

> I try to provide intimacy by being near him. I plan to end my day with reading near him when he automatically takes out his work and starts in on it like a robot. Then he jumps up and wants to make love and I say, "Wait a minute, give me time. I need more intimacy."
>
> I had to explain to him that intimacy and foreplay start a long time before going to the bedroom. It starts at breakfast, goes on at supper and sits here reading together. If he would come over here and sit beside me, that will help the intimacy, make me feel more like making love. We might not even make it up to the bedroom.
>
> He would love to make love to me all the time, but without that bonding and intimacy, even though I'm a healthy woman, I don't want sex. I want to be touched, looked at, talked to. He talks to

me maybe three minutes a day. For this I don't have to get married. The key is explaining that foreplay begins at breakfast.

Unfortunately the main reason that men are emotionally uncommunicative and thus have problems establishing intimacy with their wives is that emotional expressiveness is just the opposite of the qualities that are needed by men to succeed at work. Most men are trained to suppress emotions. Our society encourages men to be direct and forceful. Those who get ahead are those who are the most direct and forceful. So, not surprisingly, a man who has worked hard at achieving what he wants at work all day comes home and proceeds directly toward his sexual goal with his wife, not stopping for subtlety. The tenderness that she needs to respond sexually plays no part in a man's working life; indeed it must be totally repressed during his workday for him to survive. It is not surprising, then, that it is difficult for him to express it, either verbally or nonverbally, on command at night. But as we will see in Chapter 7, it is expressiveness on the part of both partners that makes a marriage vital and fulfilling. And not only does it make for a happier marriage, but according to the research done by Fernando Bartolome, expressiveness leads to self-development, which has a positive effect on professional development.*

In contrast, lack of expressiveness and communication can kill the tenderness between husbands and wives. Some women become so bitterly resentful of their husbands' attitudes that they withhold sex altogether.

He only needs me to cook his meals and wash his clothes. My bitterness has caused my needs for him sexually to arrive at a 0,

wrote the wife of a successful cattle rancher. And Louise told us:

I'm often so angry with him for coming home late that I've refused him sexually many times. Actually, our sex life is shot, rotten. We have just gotten poles apart. I don't see him enough. I don't know him anymore. I don't know what is going on in his mind. I still love my husband in a way, and I have some ingrained

---

*Must Success Cost So Much?, p. 153.

things against divorce, but he's a stranger to me and I don't sleep with strangers.

Affairs

We didn't ask our participants whether they had ever had an extramarital affair, so we have no statistics on this. But some of them volunteered the information anyway. Some, like Gail, had looked for love and sexual fulfillment outside their marriages. But, unlike Gail, who found another man at the top, most of these women sought out quite another type of man to have an affair with. Harriet said that this was true of her:

> *One question you didn't ask and maybe you should have is about affairs, since I bet they're epidemic among wives at the top. I had an affair with a man who is a musician. The thing that attracted me to him was the fact that he was strong enough to be gentle. I think it takes a hell of a strong man to show his gentle side. The intimacy I hungered for was not sexual, something my husband could never understand.*
>
> *But I know if I ever married someone else, I would be looking for a man with my husband's qualities. There is something about him and his success that is very attractive. Is that a tragic flaw in me? I guess I want to have both. I don't mean both men, but both qualities in the same man. I guess that's too much to ask for.*

For a few women, having an affair or a series of affairs was a positive solution to their problems. The wife of a diplomat, for example, recommended her "discreet and talented masseur" and enclosed his calling card with her returned questionnaire. Others felt that they were entitled to take lovers, and that this didn't affect their marriages. Unlike Gail, they apparently experienced no guilt. The thirty-eight-year-old wife of a well-known television personality, the woman who described her marriage as "perfect from the outside but lonely from the inside," fell in love with a man who was able to give her both time and attention. She told us that half the women she knows in New Jersey are having affairs with men, or women, and that this has been a major meeting ground for them. Their phone conversations and luncheons are spent discussing how great they all are at their arrangements.

But one point that the women who had had affairs made over and over was that their deepest unmet needs were more emotional than sexual. We found that this was an interesting corollary to Eda LeShan's quote from the man who said that he thought that many middle-aged men have affairs because they are really looking for a friend. In both cases sex seems to be seen as the solution to a nonsexual need. Perhaps modern society has made it easier to hop into bed with someone of the opposite sex than to really communicate with him or her. But because extramarital sex usually leads to guilt for most people, affairs were not seen as healthy or constructive by most of the women we talked to, even those who rated their marriage as poor.

Another solution to the problem of a lack of male attention that was offered by women was going out with gay men. The forty-year-old wife of a San Francisco art dealer said that this worked well for her:

> *When we first came to San Francisco and I realized that my husband's life belonged to his work, I found myself in the company of several gay men who were more than happy to escort me to various art exhibits, openings, dinner afterwards, etc. Of course in the art field there are many such men, most of whom are charming, intelligent and "safe." Since I thoroughly enjoy male company, this seemed to solve the problem of being with men but not having to worry about the sexual air of a male/female relationship.*

But after saying how bad sex at the top is, or can be, we want to underline the fact that almost a third of our participants had been able to maintain a good sex life with their husbands against all the odds. Angela spoke for many of these women when she said:

> *Obviously, when under too much pressure or fatigue there have to be adjustments or postponements, but neither of us has had a "headache" for very long!*

His Health

A majority of the women we talked to also told us that their husbands' health had been affected to some degree by the pressures of work. With the exception of one wife who asserted, "He doesn't get ulcers, he gives them," many mentioned in addition to ulcers, chronic fatigue, high blood pressure and overweight caused by eating too much rich food and lack of exercise. Many husbands smoked too much, and many drank too much, according to their wives. When asked whether her husband's health had been affected by the pressures of his work, Jane told us:

> He would say "no," I would say "yes." He suffers from stress, tension and irritability. But you know, men deny their health problems. He manifests textbook symptoms, but he does not see them as a problem, ergo, no problem. Frankly, I don't know how long he can keep this up without collapsing. But he is determined at all costs to keep going and has no use for what he calls a "pansy-ass" attitude.

Stress-related health problems seem to be more prevalent in middle managers and other professionals on the way up than they are in men who have actually arrived. According to a 1974 study by the Metropolitan Life Insurance Company, presidents and vice-presidents of companies have fewer heart attacks than those below them on the ladder.* There seem to be two possible explanations for this: first that those who have arrived at the top are survivors in the Darwinian sense, and therefore constitutionally stronger, and second that companies and organizations treat men at the top better than they do others. Executive exercise rooms, official cars and drivers, more pleasant work environments and luxurious travel arrangements all come to those who have scaled the heights. That's part of the reason others want to get there.

What can you do to help your husband cope? You can't change his work environment, but you can pick up on some of the excellent

---

*I. David Welch et al., *Beyond Burnout: How to Enjoy Your Job Again When You've Just About Had Enough* (Englewood Cliffs, N.J.: Prentice-Hall, 1982), p. 195.

suggestions made by the authors of *Beyond Burnout,* who discuss physical, intellectual, emotional, social and spiritual burnout and give helpful suggestions for men who are experiencing stress in any or all of these areas of their lives.

Your Health

Since this is a survival guide for wives of successful men, we are primarily interested in how your husband's job affects you. If you are anything like the women we surveyed, you have had some health problems, both mental and physical, at some time during your husband's successful career. The strains of coping alone, of frequent moves, of being in the public eye and of having to worry always about what others thought of them often affected the health of our participants. One woman told us that she just got stronger and stronger. But she was an exception. Many women spoke of health problems in the past. Eileen wrote:

> *When we moved to Washington, the responsibility of the family, the new job, and social obligations was overwhelming. Everyone in the family was unhappy and turned to me for help. I had about one year of severe anxiety.*

Others said that they had had both mental and physical health problems which they had overcome. A businessman's wife in Atlanta told us that she had often suffered from depression until she had learned to be more independent:

> *For a while I was very anxious about his being away from home so much, but I always hid it, and I was getting chest pains and suffered from depression. I was on Valium for a while, but I decided that I had to learn to cope myself, and I got through that period. I saw a psychiatrist for a while to help get over the problem. Because of my husband's long hours away from home, and with five children to raise, enormous burdens were placed on my shoulders which I couldn't handle.*

Many said that the hardest time for them was when the children were little. "I went through the wringer mentally when I was a lonely young mother during the long New England winters," wrote Phyllis, the professor's wife. Others, such as Jane, spoke of a problem controlling their weight:

> *I had periods of depression and put on extra weight up until about five years ago, when I became involved in and committed to aerobic exercise. I was using food to replace my husband. When he wasn't home at night, I ate to fill the void.*

Some wives drank to fill the void, with the inevitable results. Harriet told us:

> *I became an alcoholic. It developed gradually. We could afford it, so I drank it. One cocktail led to another while I sat alone waiting for him to come home to dinner.*

Most of the wives we interviewed felt that they had dealt with their health problems, but some were still struggling with physical and mental conditions which they attributed to the stresses of their husbands' success. Angela was one of these:

> *I have chronic cystitis, at times incapacitating, lower-back problems caused by stress, allergies, and you name it. I consult a psychiatrist immediately when my body gets the best of me, but I realize that there is little he can do to help me but reassure me that my health is fairly good.*
>
> *Sometimes I feel that my world is crashing down around me, but I must force myself to shove it all under the rug. I hate to trouble my husband with my worries, he has so many important things to think about. So I have recurrent bouts of aching joints, hives, and cystitis again. Such a bore.*

And Louise is still struggling with depression:

> *I have been in psychotherapy for six years. I have overdosed twice, spent a lot of time in mental wards, taken almost every psycho drug in the book and had fourteen electric shock treatments.*
>
> *My depression is chronic and it is chemical. It is presently controlled by a drug, and I think I've just about reached a decision*

to stay on this drug for life despite its disagreeable side effects.

Having said that, I will now say that because of my brain chemistry I have a tendency to be depressed whether or not things are going well. There is no way on earth I can blame my brain chemistry on my husband. But I think that my poor relationship with my husband has provided a climate in which depression flourishes, and I think our poor relationship is, for the most part, due to his making his career top priority.

Burnout

Given all these inner tensions, it is not surprising that some women do experience burnout, or the complete inability to cope. In the introduction to their book *Burn Out: The Melancholia of High Achievement,* Dr. Herbert Freudenberger and Geraldine Richelson describe people who are burned out: "Under the strain of living in our complex world, their inner resources are consumed as if by fire, leaving a great emptiness inside, although their outer shells may be more or less unchanged."* For many the feeling of burnout is short-lived, and a good cry or a generous treat to oneself helps it to pass. Others simply grit their teeth and cope because they have to; husband and children continue to make demands, and while they continue to satisfy them, the feeling of burnout goes away. But several women experienced a real crisis, or an ongoing series of crises. One of these was Jennifer:

Isn't that what this whole questionnaire is about? Not only not being able to cope successfully with my life, but often not even wanting to try. Eventually, some small crumb comes my way and I feel a little better, till next time.

I have tried to be me and the perfect congressman's wife and a homemaker in two communities and have become suicidal, irritable and impossible to live with. I was just sliding down my rope, my lifeline, less and less interested in life, and for six months I just groveled at the bottom. Death was literally the only solution I could see to any problem, large or small.

*New York: Doubleday Publishing Company/Anchor Press, 1980, p. xv.

One night I spent just lying on the bathroom floor wanting to be rescued. My husband came home and put me to bed. When someone asked me as a joke who I would want at my deathbed, I said, "My husband, if he had time."

Freudenberger and Richelson maintain that burnout is not a disgrace, that it is "a problem born of good intentions". People who experience burnout are most often committed, conscientious people who put all they have into whatever they do. That is just the trouble. They try too hard and are unable to tolerate any kind of failure. Jennifer had to be "the perfect congressman's wife," which no one could be. People who don't strive for the highest goals don't experience burnout. People who have high expectations and push themselves to meet them often do. Here is Freudenberger and Richelson's test for finding out how close *you* are to burnout. Take it, but don't worry if your score is high on the burnout scale. "Burnout is reversible, no matter how far along it is. The higher number signifies that the sooner you start being kinder to yourself, the better"

ARE YOU BURNING OUT?*

Look back over the past six months. Have you been noticing changes in yourself or in the world around you? Think of the office . . . the family . . . social situations. Allow about 30 seconds for each answer. Then assign it a number from 1 (for no or little change) to 5 (for a great deal of change) to designate the degree of change you perceive.

1. Do you tire more easily? Feel fatigued rather than energetic?
2. Are people annoying you by telling you, "You don't look so good lately?"
3. Are you working harder and harder and accomplishing less and less?
4. Are you increasingly cynical and disenchanted?
5. Are you often invaded by a sadness you can't explain?
6. Are you forgetting? (appointments, deadlines, personal possessions)

Burn Out: The Melancholia of High Achievement, pp. 17–18.

7. Are you increasingly irritable? More short-tempered? More disappointed in the people around you?
8. Are you seeing close friends and family members less frequently?
9. Are you too busy to do even routine things like make phone calls or read reports or send out your Christmas cards?
10. Are you suffering from physical complaints? (aches, pains, headaches, a lingering cold?)
11. Do you feel disoriented when the activity of the day comes to a halt?
12. Is joy elusive?
13. Are you unable to laugh at a joke about yourself?
14. Does sex seem like more trouble than it's worth?
15. Do you have very little to say to people?

THE BURNOUT SCALE

0–25	You're doing fine.
26–35	There are things you should be watching.
36–50	You're a candidate.
51–65	You're burning out.
Over 65	You're in a dangerous place, threatening to your physical and mental well-being.

Summing Up

In this chapter we have discussed some of the tensions which affect wives at the top and those on their way up. Health and sexual problems are often caused by the stresses of living with successful men. Feelings of worthlessness can lead to burnout. And burnout can lead to despair and serious depression.

Instead of offering a set of guidelines at the end of this chapter, we would like to encourage you to go right on to the next chapter of the book, Coping and Winning. Here we provide guidelines for the whole book and will, we hope, help wives at the top to survive, and to succeed.

7

COPING AND WINNING

Charlotte

One of the last interviews we did was with Charlotte, and she became the model for our concept of coping and winning. Charlotte lives in Texas, where her husband is a corporate lawyer. She and Tucker met in college. She typed legal briefs in their basement apartment while he went to law school. Now they live in the most expensive suburb of Dallas, where their Spanish-style villa is one of the highlights of the local house tour.

Charlotte is fifty-two, pleasingly plump, and speaks with a soft Texas drawl. When she told us about her thirty-year marriage to Tucker, her brown eyes shone:

> *We have an excellent marriage in that dedication and love are stronger than ever, but it's also a marriage that had to weather many adjustments and difficulties over the years. It had to grow to meet the challenges.*

We asked Charlotte what difficulties she and Tucker had overcome and how. We told her that her experiences could be of help to other wives in the same boat. We weren't interested in having someone as a role model who had never experienced pain; we wanted someone who had suffered and come through it stronger and happier, as Charlotte and her husband had.

Charlotte spoke of a time in her life several years before. Her four children were growing up and becoming independent. Her husband was at the height of his success. And she was miserable.

Tucker was running so fast that he didn't trust anyone. I saw him as a total failure as a person, unable to relate to his wife and children, or even to his own feelings. Like so many other successful men he was running as fast as he could and running scared.

I felt completely abandoned by Tucker for his job. And his job was a mistress I couldn't compete with. I started to drink too much. Two glasses of wine at night, maybe three, then four. But I never drank before five o'clock. At a party one night I asked a friend why she was drinking orange juice and she said because she was an alcoholic. I was flabbergasted. Then she looked me straight in the eye and asked me if I would go to an AA meeting with her, and I've been going ever since. It's a joy! About 5 percent of AA is about putting the cork in the bottle; the other 95 percent is how to live a better life, how to deal with anger, how to build self-esteem. It's changed my life; I needed all of these things so badly.

I wasn't a falling-down drunk. I was a kitchen drinker. I think I drank to allieviate the loneliness, the lack of companionship. I come out of the AA meetings feeling high on life instead of booze. It's a tremendous support system. There's a saying in AA that there are no strangers there, only friends you haven't met. It's a beautiful program for sharing and giving and learning and listening and growing. Sure, it has to do with drinking, but it is really about learning to like yourself again.

Before I went to AA, I didn't like myself very much. My ego was subterranean. I wouldn't have done this interview before that. Now I'm reaching out instead of hiding from life. I'm getting more involved with it and that feels good.

We asked Charlotte what Tucker had thought of her going to AA, and she said that he hadn't liked it, for two reasons. In his work and social world drinking was very important. The men drank heavily. It was professionally accepted and even encouraged. But none of his friends would have ever admitted he was an alcoholic; an alcoholic was a bum. So when Charlotte told Tucker that she was an alcoholic, it was very threatening to him, because she drank less than he did.

Also, one of the few things that Charlotte and Tucker did together in those days was drink. "It was our substitute for communication," she said. "After a couple of drinks neither of us made any sense anyway, so we really never talked."

Charlotte, like Gail, also had an affair. The other man courted her and wooed her. He was gentle and sensitive, everything that Tucker wasn't. But when Tucker found out, he was crushed. Charlotte agreed to give up her lover if Tucker would go to a marriage counselor with her. She told us that the counseling turned their marriage around, but not immediately:

> *The counseling really helped us communicate. Just having Tuck taking time out from work to be there working on our marriage meant so much to me. It made me feel important to him, something I hadn't felt for a long time. Nothing dramatic or pivotal really happened during the counseling except I went into it thinking that I wanted out of the marriage and came out of it six months later glad that I was still married.*
>
> *Even though Tuck, like so many men, had a hard time expressing his feelings, I heard and saw the love that had been there all the time. He had grown up in a home where there wasn't a lot of love or nurturing shown. I had tried, like a lot of women do, I think, to play Florence Nightingale to his emotional wounds and had failed. He didn't know how to respond, much less how to reciprocate, so I had had to get my emotional support somewhere else. But that was just an escape. Affairs and drinking are both escapes and painkillers. They only make things worse because you feel so awful about yourself the whole time.*
>
> *Tucker began to really trust the counselor, a man who had left business to go into psychology, and one day my hard-driving, successful husband said that he didn't really like that side of himself very much. He just broke down and admitted, "I don't like the corporate me. I don't like the role playing and I don't like the politics. I don't think anybody does, but there's no other way to make it professionally." Hearing him admit this really changed my feelings toward him from resentment to sympathy. I just took him in my arms and told him that it was all right, that I understood, and that he had done such a good job at such a hard thing. We were both in tears.*

Almost invariably when someone shows us that he is scared or hurting, our heart goes out to him. And everyone, men at the top included, is scared or feels pain at one time or another. In his book *Women in Transition* Dr. Andrew J. DuBrin notes, "There are cravings for warmth, understanding, tenderness and perhaps even mothering in even the most successful and hard-driving men."* Charlotte and Tucker were helped by the counselor to hear and respond to each other's deepest needs, hers for a feeling of importance, and his for encouragement and support.

But, Charlotte said, she gradually realized that she couldn't depend solely on Tucker for a feeling of importance. He alone couldn't fill that need, even if he had all the time in the world, which he didn't.

I had an empty space in me the size of the Grand Canyon and was trying to fill it with the pebbles of my husband's leftover time. It took me many months and many tears to come to the conclusion that the only thing to do was change my view of life. Only God could love me enough to fill that void. The spiritual side of AA was tremendously helpful to me, because once I felt loved by God, I was able to love myself, and that did wonders for my self-esteem.

While she was raising her four children and carrying out her social obligations as the wife of a busy and successful man, Charlotte had done volunteer work too. Over the years she had dabbled in cultural and school activities, but the volunteer job that really excited her most was working with abused children. She was horrified many times at what she saw and heard, but being able to make a difference to them and their lives gave Charlotte a tremendous sense of fulfillment. When she decided to change her view of life, she also decided to get a job. And when she thought about what she wanted to do, working with abused children had the strongest appeal. But as a volunteer she had often been frustrated by her powerlessness. Sometimes the court would order a child returned to a home situation which she knew was dangerous. So after going to law school she got a job with the county Juvenile Court, hearing cases to determine the rights and interests of abused children.

Working at something that interested her and gave her a sense

*Springfield, Ill.: Charles C. Thomas, 1972, p. 45.

of accomplishment made Charlotte a happier person. It also improved her relationship with Tucker and made her more aware of his needs. Now she understood that the work world wasn't all glamour. Her days were sometimes as long as his, and often she found it difficult to unwind too. Sharing the satisfactions and frustrations of their jobs with each other created a new bond between them. It also made them a team for the first time:

> Now I know that my opinion, even in professional matters, is taken seriously. When he asks me about things concerning his job, it's not out of politeness anymore, but because sometimes I have instincts he doesn't have or I can help him clarify his own instincts. It works in reverse too. I suddenly realized that the support has become mutual. We really respect each other's opinions. We have discovered that we are equal in every sense, and not just because we both sign the tax return.

In this chapter we will discuss the secrets of coping with marriage to a successful man and of winning rather than losing at life. We feel that the most important things are: finding and establishing your own sense of identity, developing the team concept with your husband and discovering the deeper truths of existence, which put all the small irritations and disappointments of life in their proper perspective.

Faith

When doing her research for *Pathfinders,* * Gail Sheehy found that in every group she surveyed "people of high well-being were more likely than others to speak of having a faith."

In the last chapter we talked about burnout. When we asked our participants how they kept going or recovered after feelings of burnout, many of them told us that they prayed. "Without my belief in God," said the wife of a top government official, "I could never have made it." Charlene Curry, in *The General's Lady,* † writes:

*New York: William Morrow & Company, 1981.
†Wheaton, Ill.: Tyndale House Publishers, 1981.

Time after time the Lord has taught me, until I think I've learned it forever—that whatever the Lord requires of me, he has already provided in great abundance. All I am required to do is to believe it, and to yield my life to him for whatever he wills. If I will be willing to "suit up and show up," God will be powerfully able to accomplish his plan.

Believing that she was part of God's plan made a tremendous difference to Charlene while she accompanied her husband, Jerry, to Army posts all over the world. It also helps her keep her sense of proportion now that he has become a general and she must perform as his "lady."

Not only does prayer help in times of crisis or burnout, but faith can build strong bonds within the family. Born-again Christians told us that once they put God in the center of their lives, everything else worked out. And children growing up with religious values are more secure than those without, we were told; which helped compensate for absentee fathers and material overload. A businessman's wife said that her family sponsored two Third World children, out of a desire to share some of their wealth and also to help their children see how the "real world" lives. When their son was eighteen, he spent a year working with a Christian mission in Africa. She told us:

We really encouraged this. Frankly, we couldn't bear to raise a bunch of little snobs who just lolled around the country club pool. Not that there's anything intrinsically wrong with that, but it's such a small fragment of reality. For 99.9 percent of the world it's not reality at all. I think it's depriving a child if you let him think that it is.

A return to traditional religious practices was also important to several Jewish wives whom we interviewed. Becky, the wife of a St. Louis professor, said:

My husband and I were raised in non-practicing Jewish homes. But since we've had children ourselves, we've come to realize how important religious values are. What better way to be sure that the family really gets together than to sit together around the Sabbath table. By lighting the candles and saying the prayers on Friday nights, we do something that is meaningful and brings us together.

We've also become an active part of the congregation at the temple, and this involves us with other families who share our deeper values. They have nothing to do with my husband's job and give him a very different perspective on life.

False vs. Real Cures

With faith as the cornerstone of coping, what are some of the building blocks? In their study of burnout Freudenberger and Richelson talk about false cures. Even for people who are not going through burnout, these can be tempting mechanisms. Charlotte has already named two false cures: drinking and extramarital sex. Freudenberger and Richelson, who would add drugs to this list, maintain that even without the guilt that Charlotte talked about, these releases don't satisfy our need to be in touch with our real feelings. "They take us farther and farther from ourselves," they say.*

They believe that the real cure is closeness. "Where closeness exists, burnout has a hard time staking out a claim. But closeness is in short supply these days and becoming scarcer all the time as living gets to be more and more fragmented. We cannot expect to experience it unless we actively seek it and work at it, and that isn't as easy as it may sound." But they add, "Before we can achieve closeness with others we have to achieve it with ourselves."† This is a long process and often a difficult one because often we don't want to be close to ourselves for fear of or dislike of what we find there.

Achieving closeness with ourselves demands introspection and self-knowledge. Who am I really? What do I want out of life? What am I good at? What drives me crazy? How do I want to spend the rest of my life? And once you've acquired this self-knowledge, you have to act on it. This is a two-stage process.

Self-knowledge can be arrived at on your own, or through professional counseling. In *Women in Transition,* Andrew DuBrin has a "self-knowledge questionnaire" with which you can begin the pro-

*Burn Out, p.123.
†Ibid., p. 124.

cess of finding your own identity. Another helpful book which we recommend is *Success: You Can Make It Happen,* by Dr. Lila Swell.* She includes many charts that are useful for developing self-knowledge and makes the encouraging point that most of us are *better* than we think. We really do need to think positively to avoid negative self-images. Many other books can be found in stores and libraries which will be of help in the search for self-knowledge. A list and evaluation of some of those books appear in the next chapter, Resources. We also offer suggestions as to how and where to get professional psychological counseling if this seems necessary.

Too often the women we spoke to, especially the older women, subordinated their own identities almost totally to those of their husbands. These were often the ones who told us that too much introspection was bad for you and for the people around you. We agree. Nothing is more boring than someone who is continually analyzing herself. But nothing is more ineffectual than someone who has never stopped to question herself or reflect on her life-style. We do not suggest too much introspection, just enough to set yourself on the right course if you're starting out or to correct your course if you seem headed for burnout. Change involves risk, and risk is frightening. Some people avoid looking too closely at their lives for fear that they will be disappointed by what they see. If this sounds like your situation, please do not deny the truth. Face it and change your course. All you stand to lose is your unhappiness. And once you're happier, you'll make the people around you happier too. It's not selfishness, it's selfish not to. We firmly believe that only by establishing your own identity and by validating (not apologizing for) it can you make a real success of marriage to a successful man. Again, the women we surveyed who had the best marriages were those who had the strongest sense of their own identity.

Your Identity and Identifying with Him

We asked our participants how much their identity was linked to their husbands, and how much they felt that they existed separately.

*New York: Simon & Schuster, 1977.

When we tried to answer this question ourselves, we found that it was almost impossible, so we were very impressed with the quality of the answers we received from the women we surveyed. Here are some of their responses.

The wife of an important government official told us:

> *I found my identity at twenty-six, when I met my future husband. I was really nonplussed. He was the most special person I'd ever met. I guess I hadn't realized up to that point that I wished I'd had a better education, a better background, a lot of things. The first year we went out, he was really two different personalities. One time he'd be charming, and the next time he was this other person I couldn't really understand.*
>
> *It's always been that way, and it's a challenge, but I decided that I'll never feel superior to anybody in my life and I'll never feel inferior. I suppose meeting him did this for me. I hadn't been forced to face this before.*

This woman was fortunate in that she worked out her feelings about herself before she married. Her words contrast sharply with those of another Washington wife, who said:

> *In all our dealings together, if I really pay attention to what's going on, I realize that I do not see myself as his equal. I didn't when we first married. I was treating him very much as I treated my father, and I guess I still do. I put myself in the same position as the children many times. If I need something, I'm always afraid to ask. I'm not in tandem with him.*

The first woman said that her marriage was "excellent," and the second said, "On a scale from one to ten, I'd rate my marriage as a four. We don't fight or argue, we just coexist."

Charlotte told us:

> *I know where I begin and end for the first time. Right now I am more in tune with my own persona than ever in my life. I like myself and my potential. My marriage and my relationship to my husband and my children are aspects of my identity.*
>
> *At this point I have a better sense of identity that I ever had.*

I am much less insecure and do not feel inferior. Tuck and I went on a Marriage Encounter weekend which we found out about through our church. [See Chapter 8, Resources, p. 192.] It really helped me and us. Yes, my identity is strongly linked to my husband but because that's what I want, not because I need it to be.

Sandra wrote:

Yes, I feel I have a strong sense of my own identity. But I've had to work hard at it and definitely feel more comfortable with myself than ever before. I've learned my strengths and weaknesses.

My husband and I are a pair. I wouldn't find life half as much fun if he weren't here to share it with!

Bonnie-Jean said:

To a large degree I believe I have become quite a different person because I am his wife. I never had popularity on my own, but I share his popularity. People like me because I am his wife, and this gives me the self-confidence that I was lacking. It has opened doors for me that I could never even have approached on my own.

My early life was so dismal that I cheerfully left it all behind. From the day I took John's name, I also took the identity of being his wife. At the same time I remain quite obstinately myself, and I think it is healthier in marriage for each partner to retain his or her own identity than for one to be swallowed up by the other.

This view is very different from Harriet's:

Steve would like a great deal more subservience from me. He often says his job is to make his boss look good, and he carries this out with single-minded dedication, genuinely expecting nothing for himself. I think he considers that it's my job to make him look good in the same sense, and in this I fail by having a mind of my own and asserting it from time to time. I realize, increasingly, that it is not fair to him and I should be more willing to make sacrifices for his sake. Some of the conflict in our marriage has been my failure to accept this role.

Peggy put it this way:

> *No, I don't know who I would be if I weren't Mrs. ———. I'm very comfortable sometimes with the link. At other times I wish I had my own claim to fame.*
>
> *He's so publicly liked and accepted. I'm eclipsed when being introduced. People shake my hand, but they look at him.*

While Michelle said:

> *I wish I had more self-esteem; too much of my identity was linked to my husband's. I wonder how I could have lived so long pretending I was happy.*
>
> *I do have a strong sense of my own identity [now], but I've had to work hard to develop it. I get confused by the messages that society and my upbringing have heaped on me.*
>
> *But I do feel that I have done well making a life for myself through work, children, etc. because I've had to do it almost singlehandedly, because of the almost total absence of my husband.*

There are two points made by many of the women quoted above. One is the fact that a strong sense of identity takes time to develop. This is something that one need not apologize for. A person's first identity crisis usually comes during adolescence, when the values of parents are tested against other alternatives. Many people forge their own identities then. But others—especially women—don't. Girls are more likely than boys to avoid conflict. They are raised to accept more dependence. And like Michelle, they often put a high value on being a "good girl," on not rocking the boat. Often this "good" girl goes from being dominated by her father to being dominated by her husband. If the husband is a strong, determined man, sure of what he wants in life and how to get it, her position in the relationship does not differ that much from her position vis à vis her father. "He treats me and the children the same" is a perfect expression of this. Such a wife has never developed as a separately functioning or thinking adult. At some time in her life she will have to take care of the unfinished business of developing her own identity. If she doesn't, then she is a perfect candidate for the martyr category, no matter how glamorous her life-style or how perfect the mask she presents to the outside world.

"But isn't it too late for me?" asks the fifty- or sixty-year-old. "I'd feel ridiculous acting like a teenager again, going through an identity crisis at my age. My husband would think I'd gone crazy!" He certainly would if she took on all the trappings of adolescence while she was doing it—for the same reason that a fifty-year-old man who throws over his wife and family and takes off on a motorcycle looks ridiculous. But it is not too late for her to take herself and her development seriously. Borrow the "what am I going to do when I grow up?" mentality, but leave the motorcycles and the rock music to the kids.

As we've said before, the women who had a strong sense of their own identity were happier and had better marriages. Isn't this what we all want?

After All This Introspection, Then What?

Self-knowledge is the starting point. It is the *sine qua non* of successful living, but it is not an end in itself. You must act on it. According to Helen De Rosis and Victoria Pellegrino in *The Book of Hope: How Women Can Overcome Depression:**

> Just think of what a twenty- or thirty-year-old woman would conjure up for herself if she were asked: what are you going to do with the next twenty-five years? Is a forty- or fifty-year-old woman less imaginative? She is twenty or thirty years richer in experience, in wisdom. She's twenty or thirty years more resistant to illusions and impossible expectations.
>
> If a woman in this age group wanted to do it, she could educate herself in a completely new field, and have enough time to succeed in it. That a woman hasn't started a new interest by the time she's thirty, forty, or fifty is not evidence against her starting one when she's in her fifties.

"But I'm too old to get a job, and besides my husband's job makes all sorts of demands on my time," you might say. Fine—you don't

*New York: Bantam Books, 1976, p. 231.

necessarily need a paying job (though earning your own money can do wonders for your self-esteem), and you do need to be free for your husband (though perhaps not as often as you think you do), but you do need a *center* to your life. To go back to what Jean Sisco said in Chapter 3, you need to find something that you like to do, something you do well, and something you value. After a certain age children can't meet this need. We all know the older woman who hovers around her grown children (either mentally or physically) not because they need her that much (if she's raised them well, they don't) but because she needs them. She has nothing else to fill the void in her life. And invariably she is not a happy person. We all also know the woman who goes to cooking class on Mondays, does aerobics on Tuesdays, has her hair done on Wednesdays, and works at the local hospital on Fridays. She takes Thursdays "off," but she usually spends them doing errands or paying the bills. Nothing she does is bad, everything she does is worthwhile, indeed much of it really has to be done by somebody. But she has no center. If someone asked her who she was, she'd have to ask, "On which day?"

Freud believed, and many subsequent psychologists have agreed, that two things are crucial in life, fulfilling work and fulfilling love. If you take yourself and your needs seriously, you will have to find some fulfilling work yourself. When Gail asked in despair what the answer was to her problem, she already had it, but she didn't accept it. Don't depend on another person for your happiness. Make your own. Don't waste your time or "keep busy" doing meaningless things; instead, find a center for your life, and other things will fall into their rightful place. If you find your own way to happiness, you won't need your husband to "make you happy," but you will be happier with your husband.

You as a Couple

We would now like to return to the concept of closeness as an antidote to burnout. In *Burn Out: The Melancholia of High Achievement* Freudenberger and Richelson talk about a couple who, they say, lived at cross purposes for eighteen years for the lack of a ten-minute talk. Most of us know of relationships that could have been saved or immeasurably improved had both people really said what they felt in a nonhostile way and listened to each other, if even for only ten minutes. We all avoid self-revelation at times. Some of us avoid it all the time. Since such avoidance is one of the strongest barriers to closeness, we should try to find out why we do it.

One of the main reasons is lack of trust. We don't think the other person will understand. Or he'll hate us for feeling the way we do. Thus, Freudenberger and Richelson say, "the individual writes a script in which he has constructed the other person's responses.

"Then he uses that script to condemn the person. Meanwhile, that unsuspecting other doesn't even know anything has been going on. . . . The minute we begin withholding our thoughts from others, we've begun to isolate ourselves."*

Bonnie-Jean, one of the women we interviewed who had been able to achieve a high degree of closeness with her husband, told us:

> For a long time my husband was sending me mixed messages. He'd say, "No, you don't need to entertain business contacts if you don't want to," because he knew I was shy and it was hard for me. But at the same time he'd make me feel bad because I wasn't doing it. His intentions were good, but the result was bad.
>
> Finally he let down his guard and said, "Look, it would really help me if you'd invite these people over." Instead of hearing something negative, I heard, "I need you. You are important to me," and it was much easier from that point on.

Our words often have a very different effect from the one we feared. Sometimes the effect is clearly good; of course, at other times it may not be so good, but not to risk in communication is not to communicate.

However, communication is not an end in itself but a means to closeness. If communication pushes people further apart, it is because they have different interests deep down. And if their basic interests are completely different, or antagonistic, then coexistence, much less closeness, is impossible. But we believe that in 99 cases out of 100, communication will lead to closeness, and closeness will

*Pp. 132–33.

make your marriage better. Being able to talk freely and openly with each other is essential even if some discussions are unpleasant. Too many of us have been trained to be "good wives," which means never complaining, disagreeing, voicing anger or hostility—suffering quietly.

Psychiatrists recommend certain techniques of communication. Some suggest writing your feelings down rather than voicing them. In a Marriage Encounter weekend, a time of intense communication between husband and wife, each person writes his or her feelings down in a notebook and then exchanges notebooks with his or her spouse. Writing feelings down gives one time to reflect on them and avoids interruption. And you learn to express your feelings rather than criticizing each other's behavior.

For example, if you're tired of going to official functions and having him leave you at the door, you'll achieve more by saying, "I really feel shy and lonely standing there by myself when I don't know anybody" than you will by saying, "You are so selfish and inconsiderate. You just dump me and walk away." The first makes you more vulnerable, but it also appeals to his better nature. The second makes him feel guilty and puts him on the defensive.

Another important point to remember is that feelings are neither right nor wrong; they just exist. If you don't have to apologize for your feelings, he won't have to apologize for his, and you'll both be able to relax and open up.

But what about the man who doesn't want to be close to his wife? What about the man Gail married who said, "Now that the wedding is over, our life can get back to normal. . . . I can't do my job and pay attention to you too. Good grief, find something to keep yourself busy"? He probably felt that way at the time. Most men, especially successful men, invest a great deal of themselves in their work. That's why they are successful. But they are also human. Freud's statement applies to them too: Fulfilling work *and* a fulfilling love relationship are crucial to all people. For you to be a complete person, you must find fulfilling work as well as love; for him to be a complete person, he must have fulfilling love as well as work. How do you help it happen?

There are many books written about improving your relationship with your husband. *The Secret of Staying in Love* by John Powell, S.J., is excellent, as are several others. We have an annotated list of these in our next chapter, Resources. Two things are important to remember. You must be open with your husband, and you must try to put yourself in his shoes. We have discussed openness and expressiveness before. To say it again: Tell him how you feel, and try to get him to express his feelings. Watch your timing; the end of a long, hard day is probably not the best time for a drawn-out heart-to-heart talk. Be sensitive to his rhythms and stresses, but don't let him off the hook. He needs closeness as much as you do.

Being able to truly empathize with another person is a gift, but it is a gift we can all try to get. What does it feel like to be a man who has to work all day under great stress? If he makes mistakes, they may be million-dollar ones. If he relaxes his guard, other men are ready to move in and take over. If he shows weakness, someone is sure to take advantage of it. And when he comes home, he has more demands. He must make up for lost time with his family. He must be the court of last resort for all disputes. And he mustn't complain or burden them because he's the strong one. Anyway, they wouldn't or couldn't understand. How would it feel to be him? Try it on in your mind and then think what you can do to help. He needs you, and you need him.

We're a Team

In the best marriages there is a very strong feeling of being a team. This idea can be explored on different levels. We asked our participants whether they felt that they and their husbands were a team. Many said yes.

Jean Sisco said:

> *Yes, and isn't this vital? I don't think that my husband is a workaholic like many other men I see. He is a perfectionist and a hard worker, but he has varied interests, and we like to do many things together.*

Audrey told us:

We complement each other in many ways. We do share some interests, but we've learned to enjoy each other's interests too.

And another woman wrote:

We are a team in giving money and time to community. We are still here if our son needs us. We enjoy and support public television. We're helpful to neighbors, friends and family. His collections are stamps and coins, mine are thimbles and books.

But a Senator's wife had this to say:

No, we're not because we share very little with each other. If you look at us, we both do a job. He works outside the home for money and ego gratification. I work at home taking care of all the things he doesn't have time for or interest in. I guess you could call that teamwork of a sort. I don't.

And the wife of a doctor complained:

No, and I think it's our great failure. We have spent most of our marriage pulling against each other rather than pulling together. It has troubled me all along. Thus far we have found no remedy.

Part of the problem is that we share no outside interests. There is really nothing he is interested in that we could do together. What he likes best to do is read, and this, of course, is not a togetherness project. I don't like the things he reads, so we can't even share our reading interests.

The doctor's wife speaks of herself and her husband pulling against each other rather than pulling together, and this brings us to the image of teamwork that we want to use. It is the image of two horses, joined together and pulling toward a common goal. Their appearance can be very different, but their position must be in tandem, not one behind the other. When they pull together effectively, they can achieve much more than they could singly. They complement each other.

This concept was expressed beautifully in a letter we received from Carol, who had recently attended a Marriage Encounter weekend with her husband. She sent us several pages from a notebook her husband had kept during the weekend, and we quote it here with his permission:

First, "Why did I come on this weekend?" Partially and initially because you asked me to. But then, as I thought about it, I recognized that we did need to renew our communications in our marriage because these have not been as good as they should be. At times they have been bad, so that sometimes I feel we are not sharing our daily experiences at all. I do my job and you know very little about it, and sometimes seem to care less. So I get into a cycle where I don't communicate about my job or my feelings about it or anything else, and we are sort of constipated. So there is a good reason to come on the weekend, to open up those channels again between us so that we may better share each other.

Second, "What do I like best about you?" I guess it is your warmth with people, starting obviously with me and the kids but extending beyond the family to other people. A genuine, unassuming compassion, love, whatever. It is not a feeling which comes naturally or easily to me, yet it is one I respect, admire and perhaps even envy in you. It seems to me it gives you an ease in dealing on a deeper level with other people that I lack. That quality of goodness about you makes me feel proud of you, in a moving way. When you reach out in a caring way to someone else, I feel touched and proud.

Third, "What do I like best about myself?" I guess what I like best has nothing to do with feelings (and that may be a problem) but with my intellectual and work skills, my analytical and operational abilities. They are my strengths and I am challenged by myself to use them. Actually it is my self-discipline and will power that I like best, my ability to do what I want to do whether it is in the office, jogging, cross-country skiing or whatever. Ability to put my mind and body to a task and succeed. It makes me feel fulfilled when I have done my best at something. Fulfilled and in a way drained, because I have given everything.

Fourth, "What do I like best about us?" I think that it's our ability to survive with good humor in often difficult places and circumstances. Somehow we manage, usually by recourse to humor, to break down the problems and barriers and see our way through. I like our mutual attack on the important things in life; how to raise our kids, our values, our politics. Sharing these things makes me feel comfortable, as if our home really is a psychological place, not just a physical place. I'm proud that we have coped with some very hard times, have been through some trials by fire and made it with our marriage not only intact, but stronger. It makes me feel more secure to know how much we share and how we've coped. We seem to really complement each other, at least I think we do.

This was written by one of the nation's top businessmen, extremely successful and hard driving. As he said, spending a weekend working on his marriage hadn't been his idea. But what a difference it made to his wife, and to himself, to write these things. For want of a ten-minute talk another couple had an eighteen-year misunderstanding. Thanks to ten minutes of thoughts and feelings written down in a spiral notebook, the man quoted above and his wife made a good marriage even better. Obviously it was a marriage which, like Charlotte and Tucker's, had weathered many adjustments and difficulties over the years, but it was a marriage in which husband and wife formed a team, in terms of their shared interests and values as well as their complementary qualities.

You too can have this kind of a marriage if you're willing to work on it, and on yourself. Not only will the rewards of being married to a successful man be worth the sacrifices, but you will then say, as have many of the women we talked to, "What sacrifices?"

Guidelines

1. If you think you have a problem, don't be afraid to admit it. If it's alcoholism, seek the help of AA. For other problems there are organizations that can be equally helpful.
2. Establish your own sense of identity. If you haven't done it yet, it doesn't mean that you can't start now. Don't depend on another person for your happiness. Make your own. Don't close the door

to faith; it can build strong bonds within the family. It will also help you to put the small irritations and disappointments of life into proper perspective.

3. Develop your own interests and find a center to your life.
4. Put yourself in your husband's place—try to appreciate his situation.
5. Develop a team concept with your husband. A trusted counselor or therapist can help you and your husband to rebuild your marriage if you both have the motivation.
6. Communication is a means to closeness. Talk to your husband about your feelings and needs. Feelings are neither right nor wrong. You don't have to apologize for them. Tell him how you feel and get him to express his feelings. He needs closeness as much as you do.

The twelve people quoted in this section have not been discussed in the text of this book and no connection should be made between their names and the descriptions appearing in the text.

RESOURCES

WORDS OF WISDOM
*From a Dozen Well-Known Wives at the Top
Who Have Coped and Won*

1. "To put it bluntly, don't be a martyr or anyone's doormat!"
   —Dottie Blackmun,
   wife of the Supreme Court Justice

2. "To put on an act creates pressure that will build up, and finally blow up. Be yourself."
   —Peatsy Hollings,
   wife of the U.S. Senator

3. "I would advise any woman who feels she cannot deal with the exigencies of success to seek help, either from a religious leader or from a professional therapist."
   —Barbara A. Phillips,
   *wife of the chairman and Chief
   Executive Officer of Dow Jones & Company*

4. "The best advice I could give is to be open, active and organized."
   —Deborah Toll,
   *wife of the president of the
   University of Maryland*

5. "When friends complain about making train connections to New York, I say, 'You're lucky you're not on a cattle car going to Siberia.'"
   —Mary Ann Warner,
   *wife of the Chief Executive Officer
   of Mobil Corporation*

6. "The worst thing in the world is making comparisons. Everyone is an individual. Be grateful for what you have and don't dwell on what you don't. From time to time try to remember why you married him in the first place."

> —Pat Haig,
> *wife of the former Secretary of State*

7. "When traveling, take advantage of the time to see and learn, don't waste it shopping."

> —Betsey C. Caldwell,
> *wife of the Chief Executive Officer of Ford Motor Company*

8. "Everyone should be themselves more than anything else. You'll be doing others a service. This helped me survive the pressures of our four years at the White House."

> —Musha Brzezinski,
> *wife of the former head of the National Security Council*

9. "Try church!"

> —Barbara Bush,
> *wife of the Vice-President of the United States*

10. "I always encourage my students and patients to develop a strong identity of their own rather than to be satisfied identifying with husband or children or neighborhood, etc."

> —Madeline E. Lacovara,
> *wife of the counsel to the Watergate Special Prosecutor*

11. "Discover what you want to be and do, what you already do well, and set a path for fulfillment that is mindful of the other demands around you but not subordinate to them."

> —Sharon Frink,
> *married to U.S. Congressman Ottinger*

12. "His success has given us an interesting, exciting life with many opportunities to learn and experience things, broadening and growing together into better people."

> —Sally D. Danforth,
> *wife of the U.S. Senator*

And finally we would like to pass on this thought:

"Whenever you feel that life is unfair, consider the plight of the wife of the migrant worker, who never has a home of her own, moves constantly, remains poor, works hard, never sees a way to improve life for her children, and sleeps every night with an exhausted, dejected man."

—Anonymous

BOOKS

These books and organizations have been recommended by the women who took part in our study. We in turn recommend them to you.

1. *Marriage*

Dreikurs, Rudolf, M.D. *The Challenge of Marriage.* New York: Hawthorn Books, 1946.

This book is a classic of marriage counseling literature. Written thirty-eight years ago, its message is as valid today as it was then. Dreikurs asserts, "The willingness to cooperate can overcome every obstacle, and without this fundamental willingness minor obstacles can become overwhelming." He also states that any "outlook on life based on faith and confidence—religious or secular—increases aptitude and competence for harmonious cooperation and generates an atmosphere of genuine kindness and tolerance."

Dreikurs is an eminent authority on parenting and child rearing as well as marriage counseling.

Kiev, Ari, M.D. *How to Keep Love Alive.* New York: Harper & Row, 1982.

Noted author and psychiatrist Ari Kiev contends that conflict in marriage is not necessarily a bad thing. One must understand conflict and learn how to deal with it constructively. Even more important is recognizing the negative patterns and roles that people act out which bring conflict into their lives. Once these patterns are broken, conflicts can be resolved.

Dr. Kiev emphasizes the importance of "learning to talk with each other" and says that "it is unrealistic to expect your partner to know exactly what you want without being briefed periodically by you." He provides case studies of couples who have confronted their differences rather than avoided them and have thus enriched their partnership rather than diminished it. "Growth in a relationship depends not on sameness, but, ironically, on unevenness: on variety and mutation and trouble."

LeShan, Eda. *The Wonderful Crisis of Middle Age.* New York: David McKay Company, 1973.

Eda LeShan calls Erich Segal a "coward." "It's a real cop-out to kill off the young wife [in *Love Story*] while they are still in the first blush of romance

... it would have taken a lot more courage to let them live through marriage-in-middle-age!"

LeShan discusses the problems faced by a couple when children leave home and the strain of sustaining a marriage without the bonds of parenthood. She also points out the pluses and minuses of extramarital affairs. Often, she believes, they can lead to a better marriage, depending on how they are handled. Her conclusion: "Where there are still strong ties of caring and where the couple have the courage to face the implications of an affair, marriages almost invariably are improved by the crisis."

Powell, John, S.J. *The Secret of Staying in Love.* Allen, Tex.: Argus Communications, 1974.

This is a beautiful book by the author of *A Reason to Live! A Reason to Die!* and *Why Am I Afraid to Tell You Who I Am?* Powell is a professor of both psychology and theology at Loyola University. He believes in divine and human love, maintaining that love is the one thing that can heal psychological wounds and bring about change and growth.

In the first part of this book Powell discusses the problems of self-doubt and self-hate. He says that these two villains have distorted and destroyed many relationships. Only the love of a one-to-one relationship can restore self-confidence and self-love. And only if we can love ourselves can we truly love another.

In the second part of the book the author talks about "the anatomy of effective love." He believes that real love is an unconditional commitment between two people. He talks about identifying and expressing feelings and about the necessity of dialogue, the sharing of feelings between two people in love. *The Secret of Staying in Love* ends with a list of dialogue topics. Couples who have attended a Marriage Encounter weekend will find that many of Powell's ideas are used there.

Rubin, Lillian B. *Intimate Strangers.* New York: Harper & Row, 1983.

In this book psychotherapist Dr. Rubin takes a close look at relationships between women and men. Through interviews she conducted over many years, she gained deep insights into the different attitudes men and women have toward intimacy. Dr. Rubin attributes these differences to the woman's primary role as nurturer and explains how this affects such critical areas as sexuality, dependency, work and parenting. She says that in many cases the avoidance of talking about feelings makes intimacy almost impossible to attain: "Trying to explain to me the one thing she thought most important in her 34-year marriage, one woman said almost casually, 'It's worked so well because we both keep very busy and we don't see that much of each other.' "

Lillian Rubin asks her interviewees questions about the most intimate aspects of their lives. The fresh and honest responses of her patients hit close to home. Dr. Rubin doesn't offer easy solutions, but she raises many important and helpful questions.

Shain, Merle. *When Lovers Are Friends.* New York: Bantam Books, 1979.

This is a book about love, friendship and truth. Although not specifically a book to build marriages, *When Lovers Are Friends* is about the importance of friendship, between men and women in general as well as husbands and wives. Shain believes that many couples worry needlessly that friendships outside a marriage threaten the marriage. She maintains that if "we had more friendships, we'd have fewer marriages which break up and a lot of mates who might have strayed before would be content to remain at home. Friendships make marriages more stable by giving the partners a place to air ambivalences without threatening anyone."

Shain talks about how to establish friendships and how to keep them alive. "Even if you find a friend who is less than perfect, you'll come out of a friendship enriched."

2. *Children*

Dodson, Fitzhugh, M.D. *How to Father.* New York: New American Library/
    Signet, 1975.

This is a comprehensive guide to child rearing aimed particularly (but not exclusively) at fathers. Dodson describes in great detail the various stages of childhood, from infancy to adolescence. He explains the physical as well as the emotional development of the child and advises parents how best to deal with particular problems and how to enhance a tense or strained relationship with a child.

Dodson suggests that as children become older, it is important for a father to be able to admit he has made mistakes: "If you made mistakes, don't be afraid to admit them to your child. You might say 'Larry I guess I was too busy with my work when you were younger, and I didn't spend enough time with you, but things will be different now,' or 'Betty, I think I have been expecting too much of you as a child. I guess I've been expecting you to act more like a grown-up, but I'm beginning to see things a little differently now."

Hersh, Steven P. *The Executive Parent.* New York: Simon & Schuster/
    Sovereign Books, 1979.

This book, written by an eminent Washington psychiatrist, deals with the particular problems of busy, preoccupied men and their often neglected families. Hersh is sympathetic with the plight of such people: "For some executives, years flash by, even a lifetime, without their being much aware of the distance they have put between themselves and such important others as spouse and children. Without empathy, without pity, and without ultimate gratitude (despite salaries and special awards) the system voraciously demands more and more."

Hersh suggests that executives can arrange their lives so that they can meet their responsibilities and have freedom too. Serious problems with children can be avoided by better communication between fathers and their families. A father should "dress up" his day and thereby make it more interesting to his family and himself. And his family should be sensitive to his state of mind when he comes home at night.

Losoncy, Lewis E. *Turning People On: How to Be an Encouraging Person.*
    Englewood Cliffs, N.J.: Prentice-Hall, 1977.

This book is a very useful tool for motivating a discouraged child or anyone else. It is really a guide to re-energizing people who need a lift and it's written for teachers, social workers and psychologists as well as parents.

Some of the questions the author asks are: "What is the raw material of the encouragement process?" "What is often the reason for feelings of boredom and lassitude?" "What single element promotes resistance to risk-taking in a discouraged person?" He encourages the reader to find answers to these questions and others.

Marks, Jane. *Help: A Guide to Counseling and Therapy Without a Hassle.* New York: Dell Publishing Company, 1976.

This is a book written expressly for the teenage reader. It dispels the myth that you must be crazy to go to a shrink. Often neither parents nor friends have the training and qualifications to help a teenager in trouble. Lack of patience and experience as well as emotional involvement disqualify them.

Marks describes the functions of a therapist, a psychiatrist, a psychologist and a social worker. She looks at group and family therapy and explains in detail how to go about getting help and what to expect as a result of treatment and counseling. Her list of options allows teenagers to seek and find help on their own, thus enabling them to gain control over their own lives.

Narramore, Bruce, M.D. *Help! I'm a Parent.* Grand Rapids, Mich.: Zondervan Publishing House, 1972.

Based on both biblical and psychological truths, this book offers a solid and consistent basis for child rearing. Narramore begins by asking the question "Why is it that well-meaning, loving parents have children who are uncooperative and maladjusted?" and answers it by saying that the reason they do is because they have "learned maladaptive patterns of reacting to other family members."

Help! I'm a Parent is a manual designed to improve parents' understanding of their children and to help them encourage positive growth and development.

Tec, Leon, M.D. *The Fear of Success.* New York: New American Library/Signet, 1978.

The fear of success can be as severe and as strong as the fear of failure. Tec, a child psychiatrist, recognizes this fear even in those "who ostensibly have succeeded and reached the top of their fields." Parents can inflict this crippling fear on children, and Tec deals extensively with the success fears of children and their reluctance to grow up (the Peter Pan syndrome) and suggests constructive ways for parents to help them solve their problems.

3. *Careers*

Alter, JoAnne. *A Part-time Career for a Full-time You.* Boston: Houghton Mifflin Company, 1982.

An excellent reference book, primarily aimed at women in search of a part-time job—"whether that individual is a student, a woman at home with young children or seeking to re-enter the work-force after a long absence

. . . a person approaching retirement age, or someone looking for time to pursue educational, professional, recreational activities."

Alter provides up-to-date statistics, anecdotes, case histories and an extensive reading list for serious job hunters. She lists federal government agencies that have national part-time placement programs as well as the twenty-five top American companies that hire part-time workers.

She paints a realistic picture of the part-time job market and rates today's best part-time jobs. She includes a chapter on job sharing and freelance work and has a very good chapter on work "from or in your home."

Behr, Marion, and Wendy Lazar. *Women Working Home: The Homebased Business Guide and Directory.* Scarsdale, N.Y.: WWH Press, 1981.

There are many reasons why some women want to work at home. The main ones are that mothers "are anxious to be present when their children return home from school, low overhead, no need to commute, and having materials readily accessible at all hours of the day and night."

This book explores all the important aspects of working at home. The authors have interviewed hundreds of women with successful home-based businesses and compiled a handy reference tool for any woman who wants to turn a hobby into a business.

A list of the ten top professions practiced at home, as well as a directory by state which lists 111 different occupations nationwide, are included.

Bolles, Richard Nelson. *What Color Is Your Parachute? A Practical Manual for Job Hunters & Career Changers.* Berkeley, Cal.: Ten Speed Press, 1982.

An excellent guide for job hunters. Bolles explains in great detail how to go about finding and applying for a job. His exercises and charts, designed to help you find out exactly what you want, make this book a treasure of information. "You have to know what it is you want, or someone is going to sell you a bill of goods somewhere along the line that can do irreparable damage to your self-esteem, your sense of worth, and your stewardship of the talents that God gave you," he asserts. He covers the entire spectrum from career starters to career changers and advises how to do it without professional help. His constant reassurances that you can do it, supplemented with a wide range of reference materials, practical exercises and a "Quick Job Hunting Map," make this book a pleasurable and invaluable source for anyone wanting a job or a career.

The staff of Catalyst. *Making the Most of Your First Job.* New York: G.P. Putnam's Sons, 1981.

"If you are a woman 'entering (or reentering)' the paid labor force after having been home for several years, you're probably also worried about being able to juggle mother, wife, and job responsibilities." This book relieves many of the fears women experience when they decide to get a job. The authors encourage you to examine your uneasy feelings, your worries and your guilt, write them down and discuss them with your family and women in similar situations; they offer suggestions as to how to minimize many of your problems; they also tell you all you need to know about business etiquette and give useful advice on how to deal with colleagues, cope with office politics and intrigues on the job, develop a good writing style, evaluate your potential and quit your job with tact.

The book contains an extensive bibliography.

Fisher, Roger, and William Ury of the Harvard Negotiating Project. *Getting to Yes: Negotiating Agreement Without Giving In.* New York: Penguin Books, 1983 (first published by Houghton Mifflin Company, 1981).

Getting to Yes provides the reader with the tools necessary to settle arguments and deal with differences without giving in or letting the other side lose face. "Everyday families, neighbors, couples, employees, bosses, businesses, consumers, salesmen, lawyers and nations face this same dilemma of how to get to yes without going to war." The authors have devised a negotiating system which can be applied to everyday domestic arguments as well as high-level business negotiations, "by United States diplomats in arms control talks with the Soviet Union, and by couples in deciding everything from where to go for vacation to how to divide their property if they get divorced."

The key to the system is to avoid emotional involvement. "Anger and resentment often result as one side sees itself bending to the rigid will of the other while its own legitimate concerns go unaddressed." Fisher and Ury show how to "separate the people from the problem, focus on interests, not positions, invent options for mutual gain, and insist on mutual criteria." Their method stresses the importance of communication. "Without communication there is no negotiation."

Kirsch, Richard K. *Go Hire Yourself an Employer.* Garden City, N.Y.: Doubleday Publishing Company/Anchor Press, 1973.

"If you want an interesting job, find it in the hidden job market where favoritism, whimsey, and sheer capriciousness reign. Jobs frequently, as you would expect, are where the money is." Kirsch's book, based on his experience as vice-president of a talent search firm, advises avoiding employment agencies like the plague and staying away from the personnel departments of companies; but he recommends that you "interview *everyone* about *where* you can find the job you want. Don't interview for a job—INTERVIEW FOR INFORMATION. . . ." "You stake out the key people in each company, the men and women you would want to work for and from whom you can learn, and ask their advice on how to move up in your field."

If you have no qualification in the field in which you want to work, Kirsch suggests volunteering for no pay and waiting for a lucky break. "Volunteer work—especially in glamour jobs such as the theater, communications, and political action—is useful training and makes the volunteer, especially if he becomes rapidly indispensable, highly visible to decision makers who are quick to recognize and promote competence."

4. *Special People, Special Problems*

Evans, Paul L., and Fernando Bartolome. *Must Success Cost So Much?* New York: Basic Books, 1981.

Must the price of corporate success inevitably be divorce, estranged children, ulcers and a coronary? For some the answer seems to be yes. Yet others, with no obvious advantage, cope with the toughest demands and still lead full lives outside the office. Evans and Bartolome, both international management experts, interviewed hundreds of executives and analyzed their success or failure as professionals, husbands and fathers. They assert: "Behind every great man stands a great relationship." And they believe that one of the partners in this relationship must be a woman who deals with her own development needs.

Friedman, Meyer, M.D., and Ray H. Rosenman, M.D. *Type A Behavior and Your Heart.* New York: Random House/Ballantine-Fawcett, 1982.

Every wife of a successful man should read this excellent manual, or better still, get her husband to read it. Well written, sometimes witty, always informative, *Type A Behavior and Your Heart* makes it clear that it is not the socioeconomic position of a man or woman which determines whether he or she is "Type A." "Type A behavior can be observed in any person who is aggressively involved in a chronic, incessant struggle to achieve more and more in less and less time, and if required to do so, against the opposing efforts of other things or other persons."

Friedman and Rosenman believe that it is never too late to change from Type A behavior to the more healthy Type B. They give excellent advice concerning dietary changes (a daily food plan with dos and don'ts is included) as well as philosophical guidelines for a changed outlook on life.

Greiff, Barrie S., M.D., and Preston K. Munter, M.D. *Tradeoffs: Executives, Family, and Organizational Life.* New York: New American Library, 1980.

This book describes the stages of the executive career, starting with the dilemmas facing young executives and covering executive women, dual-career families, minority group members and executives in mid-life. It is an authoritative guide to the trade-offs which can make the executive life a harmonic whole rather than a balancing act.

The authors state: "Some executives *need* a dependent, leaning wife. She satisfies their need for power and control, possibly serving as a balance for what they may lack in their jobs. But somewhere along the line this is likely to backfire. Many women recognize that they have subjugated their own needs to those of their husbands, whereby losing their independence and sacrificing their individuality and limiting their own growth. They often suffer severe loss of self-esteem and become angry and depressed. Some are aware of this but make the tradeoff in order to be the 'boss's wife.' Others rebel and assert their independence, breaking out of the marriage. . . . Another group strikes a balance . . . that means both husband and wife must make reasonable tradeoffs that respect each other's needs and the reality of the work situation."

Levinson, Daniel J., M.D., with Charlotte Darrow, Edward B. Klein, Maria H. Levinson and Braxton McKee. *The Seasons of a Man's Life.* New York: Alfred A. Knopf, 1978.

For this book Levinson and his team interviewed and analyzed forty men in different professions such as business, labor, writing and science. Their study reveals that there is a definite age-linked timetable of change and often crisis in men, explaining why men "frequently change jobs, and sometimes wives at particular stages of life."

The interviews, which were conducted over a long period of time, begin when a man enters the work world, cover the settling-down period, continue as he approaches a mid-life transition and conclude with an in-depth analysis of each life cycle. The authors find that "only after we understand the profound significance of the epochs in our lives, can we understand the ways in which one is, at a single time, a child, a youth, a middle-aged and elderly person. We are never ageless."

Machlowitz, Marilyn. *Workaholics: Living with Them, Working with Them.* Reading, Mass.: Addison-Wesley Publishing Company, 1980.

Some, but not all, successful men can be catagorized as workaholics. Marilyn Machlowitz calls them "work junkies," who love their work and live their work. She concludes that the majority of the workaholics that she interviewed seemed happy and fulfilled in their lives. However, she found that most of their wives didn't.

Machlowitz advises people who are married to workaholics to recognize the behavior as an addictive one but to try to maximize the pleasures and minimize the pressures of life with such a person.

Mayer, Nancy. *The Male Mid-life Crisis: Fresh Starts After 40.* New York: New American Library/Signet, 1970.

This book offers some interesting insights into the changes which take place in men after age forty. Mayer interviewed two hundred men for this study, men who were not typical or average, but "who are in some way special men who have lived deeply and daringly." She examines the trend to drop out at mid-life and believes that it represents either a rebellion against existing norms or a search for a better, more fully human life.

5. *Outer Stresses*

Burns, David, M.D. *Feeling Good: The New Mood Therapy.* New York: William Morrow & Company, 1980.

This is a constructive and helpful book about depression. Burns has developed a technique which he says can help anybody conquer depression. His problem-solving and coping techniques (cognitive therapy) are applicable to every crisis in modern life, from minor irritations to major emotional collapse. This includes concrete problems, such as divorce, death and failure, as well as those vague chronic problems that seem to have no obvious external cause, such as lack of self-confidence, frustration and apathy. Burns explains how to diagnose moods and explains why people feel "high" and "low" at different times.

He furnishes many role-playing models, draws on his extensive experience as a psychiatrist and comes up with a host of workable resolutions for almost every possible situation. This is a rewarding book that leaves the reader feeling good.

De Rosis, Helen A., M.D., and Victoria Y. Pellegrino. *The Book of Hope: How Women Can Overcome Depression (and Loneliness, Anxiety, Shyness, Boredom, and Inertia).* New York: Bantam Books, 1977.

Authors De Rosis and Pellegrino interviewed hundreds of women for this book: wives and mothers who were bewildered and hurt by their husbands' demands for a "more interesting" marriage; ambitious business women who simply couldn't face another day of sadness and frustration; women who found themselves unable to enjoy and sustain sexual relationships; women who felt guilty for not having any fun with their children. The authors discovered that most of these women suffered from "low grade depression" and not just from "dissatisfaction and restlessness," as they had believed.

In a variety of interesting case studies the authors describe the symptoms of low-grade depression and analyze the possibilities available to the women affected. They explain the cause of depression and tell the reader "how you can reclaim your rightful heritage, your right to be yourself, your right to a satisfying life, your right to grow, your right to decide your life goals."

Forbes, Rosalind, Ed.D. *Life Stress: How to Manage Stress in Your Life and Make It Work for You.* New York: Doubleday Publishing Company, 1979.

"Stress cannot be eliminated from daily life, nor should it. However, it can and should be managed so that it enhances rather than diminishes our productivity, interpersonal relationships, and the general zest for living," writes Rosalind Forbes in the preface to this book. She conducts workshops in handling stress which are held nation-wide.

Forbes's book is short and readable and contains many tests and exercises such as: "How High Is Your Stress Level?" "How to Tell If You're a Stress-Prone Personality" and "Twenty-one Day Plan to Break the Stress-Prone Rut." She also gives specific advice on dealing with moves, making the home more tranquil and helping children deal with stress. Her chapter entitled "Spouses of Superachievers" will be particularly useful for wives at the top.

Freudenberger, Herbert J., M.D., and Geraldine Richelson. *Burn Out: The Melancholia of High Achievement.* New York: Doubleday Publishing Company/Anchor Press, 1980.

This is a well-written and perceptive analysis of burnout, what it is and what to do about it. Using many real-life examples, the authors discuss "false" cures for burnout and suggest a true cure. They also point to the signs of burnout and suggest ways of stopping it before it becomes a threat to mental and physical health.

The authors write, "There are many specific steps you can take to interrupt a burnout and get yourself headed toward a more rewarding life. . . . That fire which should be burning so bright inside of you is consuming, rather than warming you."

Scarf, Maggie. *Unfinished Business: Pressure Points in the Lives of Women.* New York: Doubleday Publishing Company, 1980.

A thorough and exhaustive study of depressed women, *Unfinished Business* starts with the case of a seventeen-year-old girl who underwent a saline abortion and then refused to leave the hospital because she had nowhere to go. Scarf traces the lives of many women from their teens through their twenties and thirties and into their sixties. She sheds light on why and when a woman is likely to break down and what crucial factors are apt to be involved.

Scarf attributes depression mainly to the loss of relationships and encourages women to learn to become more independent. She concludes: "Depression has been called the common cold of psychiatric disorders. What must be remembered, in this particular instance, is that it is a cold for which powerful cures now do exist."

Welch, I. David, Donald C. Medieros, and George A. Tate. *Beyond Burnout: How to Enjoy Your Job Again When You've Just About Had Enough.* Englewood Cliffs, N.J.: Prentice-Hall, 1982.

This book about burnout also discusses who gets it and why. Part I breaks down the burnout-prone by profession: teachers, doctors, nurses, executives and clergymen are included. Unfortunately, wives of successful men do not appear on their list. Still, it is helpful for wives to read about burnout from their husbands' work and sometimes their own. In Part II there are specific activities recommended for combating burnout which can also be used as preventive measures.

One of the conclusions that Welch, Medieros and Tate draw is this: In order to reverse the process of burnout, people need to recognize their own contribution to their plight; they are part of the problem. That is the negative side. The positive side is that they are also part of the solution.

6. *Inner Tensions*

Baruch, Grace, Rosalind Barnett and Caryl Rivers. *Lifeprints: New Patterns of Love & Work for Today's Women.* New York: McGraw-Hill, 1983.

Lifeprints is a sociological study of women's attitudes about work, marriage and children, an interesting, highly readable approach to the old question "What makes women happy?" The authors conclude that women need to develop both the work and family sides of their lives for well-being. "Many researchers think that it is precisely because most men function in both spheres —family and work—that their mental health has tended to be better than women's." The authors make an interesting point about the correlation between the amount of money women contribute to the family income and their sexual satisfaction. A woman who earns good money feels good about herself, and "the better you feel about yourself, the more you are able to take steps toward enjoyable sexual relationships."

Lifeprints breaks down many of the traditional myths about marriage such as: being married is a guarantor against depression; marriage ensures a sense of self-esteem, marriage makes women feel in control of their lives. The book stresses the importance of communication and support between partners, pointing out that "one can't be loving and open with bottled-up anger inside."

Bloom, Lynn Z., Karen Coburn and Joan Pearlman. *The New Assertive Woman.* New York: Delacorte Press, 1975.

"The assertive woman makes her own choices, is usually confident and feels good about herself . . . she usually achieves her goals, and even when she doesn't she still feels good. She expresses her feelings, needs and ideas, standing up for her legitimate rights in ways that don't violate the rights of others."

This helpful and encouraging book provides the tools for any woman to develop her own personality. Becoming assertive without turning aggressive can be invaluable to a woman who is in the process of deciding to make changes in her life. It may also help deal with logistics of "juggling family, home and a new role without going under."

The authors discuss everyday problems and solutions in terms of the training groups they have conducted. This makes it easy for the reader to identify with the people in the book and eager to go out and try herself. Role playing, models, questionnaires, charts, guidelines and checklists actively involve the reader and enable her to apply newfound skills to her own unique situation.

Carnegie, Dale. *How to Win Friends and Influence People.* New York: Pocket Books, 1936.

One of the original "self-help" books, *How to Win Friends and Influence People* gives time-tested advice that has helped thousands of men and women to maximize their potential. While the title has almost become a cliché, Carnegie's advice is simple and easy to apply. Modern-day gurus build on his theory that "you can take any situation you're in . . . and make it work for you!" A classic, this book is easy to read, and reread.

Dyer, Wayne W., M.D. *Pulling Your Own Strings.* New York: Avon Books, 1979.

At the core of this entertaining book is the conviction that all people have the power to choose between being happy or sad, victor or victim, and that each of us has the innate potential to achieve greatness. Dyer asserts: "If you want to work at something, and you are willing to ignore the way you're 'supposed to do it' or the way 'everybody else does it' and get on with doing it your way, with the expectation that you'll eventually succeed, then you will."

The author's positive attitude encourages the reader to look within herself for ways to turn her life around. By developing a position of strength and becoming more assertive, he believes that you can teach others how you want to be treated. There are tests accompanying each chapter which allow the reader to evaluate her own situation.

James, Muriel, and Dorothy Jongeward. *Born to Win: Transactional Analysis with Gestalt Experiments.* Reading, Mass.: Addison-Wesley Publishing Company, 1971.

This book is primarily concerned with the theory of Transactional Analysis and its application in the daily life of the average person. The reader learns a rational method of analyzing and understanding behavior. Bosses can improve their interaction with subordinates, parents with children, and husbands and wives can learn to talk to each other and how to "fight fair."

Exercises and experiments following each chapter are designed to assist the reader in applying the theory. A thoroughly readable and workable book, *Born to Win* offers excellent guidelines for making the transition from "total helplessness to independence."

Peale, Norman Vincent. *Dynamic Imaging: The Powerful Way to Change Your Life.* Old Tappan, N.J.: Fleming H. Revell Company, 1982.

An exciting book by the author of the well-known *Power of Positive Thinking, Dynamic Imaging* takes Dr. Peale's theory one step further. He believes that not only will positive thinking bring about positive results in a person's life but that imagining a desired outcome in full-colored detail puts into play powerful forces to bring it about.

Chapters include: "How Imaging Helps to Bolster a Shaky Ego," "Use Imaging to Outwit Worry" and "Imaging the Tenseness Out of Tension," as well as many others. This is a wonderfully uplifting book!

7. Coping and Winning

Curry, Charlene. *The General's Lady.* Wheaton, Ill.: Tyndale House Publishers, 1981.

Although she is now the wife of one of America's top generals, Charlene Curry has experienced military life at the bottom. Starting their marriage in the town of McKeesport, Pennsylvania, secure in their love for each other and in their faith in God, Jerry and Charlene traveled far, both geographically and spiritually. Separations often put Jerry in the Far East while Charlene and the children managed as best they could in temporary housing on another continent. During some of the hardest times, Charlene admits, she had serious health problems as well as a violent temper due to the stress and strain of their life-style.

A home leave in the States and the prayers of Jerry's mother led both Charlene and Jerry to accept baptism in the Holy Spirit, and from that point on their lives were transformed. As Charlene describes this experience, "I sensed that life was about to unfold in such fullness I would hardly be able to take it in. Even after I went to bed that night, I could still sense the Holy Spirit's presence throughout my entire being. When I awoke the next morning I felt like a brand-new person. All the old strivings in me had vanished, for the time being at least. I had been trying to live without the spirit that gives life. No wonder it hadn't worked. With the Spirit, instead of feeling afraid I wouldn't measure up, I knew I could do all things. Only it wouldn't be Charlene Curry who was doing them. It would be the Holy Spirit in me, living the victory Jesus had won on the Cross."

Jungreis, Esther. *The Jewish Soul on Fire: A Remarkable Woman Shows How Faith Can Change Your Life.* New York: William Morrow & Company, 1982.

In her crusade to bring non-committed Jews back to the faith of their fathers, Rebbetzin Esther Jungreis (wife of the rabbi) has reached and touched many Jews who had fallen away from the traditions of Judaism. She examines the American Jewish experience, which in many cases has led to assimilation and intermarriage for lack of clear role models.

As a counselor she helps young women find the right balance between motherhood and their careers, using the Bible as a guide. Her anecdotes illustrate clearly the malaise of today's modern Jewish society: "In my home town if a man failed to show up at synagogue we knew something was wrong. But here, it's just the opposite. If I see a new face at services, I know there is trouble. Either someone is ill, dying or undergoing a personal crisis, for why else would he come to pray?"

Lewis, C. S.. *The Case for Christianity,* 24th printing. New York: Macmillan Publishing Company, 1975.

The popularity of this little book is a testimony to its excellence. In simple but intellectual terms C. S. Lewis presents the case for Christianity. Building on the concept of "right and wrong as the clue to the meaning of the universe," the author writes " . . . we know that if there does exist an absolute goodness, it must hate most of what we do. That's the terrible fix we're in. If the universe is not governed by an absolute goodness then all our efforts are in the long run hopeless. But if it is, then we are making ourselves enemies to that goodness every day, and aren't in the least likely to do any better tomorrow, and so our case is hopeless again." Christianity offers a way of putting ourselves right with this "goodness" through the saving power of Jesus Christ.

Marshall, Catherine. *The Helper.* Lincoln, Va.: Chosen Books Publishing Company, 1978.

Written by one of the most popular Christian authors in America, *The Helper* focuses on the third person of the Trinity, the Holy Spirit. Marshall examines the nature of the Holy Spirit and answers the question "How do I receive Him?" She believes that the Spirit guides and protects us every day.

The Helper includes forty prayers and biblical readings, making it ideal for Lenten study.

Powell, John, S.J. *A Reason to Live! A Reason to Die!: A New Look at Faith in God.* Allen, Tex.: Argus Communications, 1972.

John Powell writes, "Only the eyes of faith can see beneath the surface of things, and only the hope of faith gives a coherence to the disparate aspects of human existence. It deepens us not only in our unity with God but in our unity with another."

A Reason to Live! A Reason to Die! puts God and faith in the center of man's life. It explores contemporary man's search for identity as well as the anatomy of faith itself. Powell believes that building faith is a long, slow and sometimes painful process, but that maturity of faith is worth all the effort.

Timmons, Tim. *Loneliness Is Not a Disease.* New York: Ballantine Books, 1981.

Tim Timmons believes that nobody is condemned to loneliness: "It is a decision, not a disease and it can be eliminated by the positive decision to love and be loved." In this thoughtful study the author of *Maximum Marriage* analyzes various aspects of loneliness. He acknowledges that loneliness can kill and that dying of a broken heart is not a myth. He distinguishes between being "alone," which is a physical separation, and being "lonely," which is a spiritual separation. While it is important to be alone, it can be crippling and debilitating to be lonely. Alcohol, drugs and television bring only temporary relief from this "suicide in slow motion," and so does over-involvement with ourselves.

Timmons believes that moving from loneliness to love is a positive step which is difficult but possible. Helping, healing, touching and caring are all ingredients of this therapeutic book, a book which can help you find new ways to yourself and to God.

ORGANIZATIONS

Professional Organizations
> Military wives' clubs
> Doctors' wives' clubs
> Foreign Service wives' clubs
> Young presidents' clubs and many others

These can be a helpful support system for your special needs as they relate to your husband's job.

Civic Organizations
> U.S. Jayceettes
> Junior League
> League of Women Voters

These can help you orient yourself in a new community as well as be a source of friends. Check your phone book for location and phone numbers.

Religious Organizations

Marriage Encounter: Though not connected with any specific church, the Marriage Encounter movement is religious in orientation. Its goal is to "make good marriages better." Catholic, Protestant and Jewish groups can be found in most cities. Try looking under "Marriage Encounter" in the phone book, or ask your priest, minister or rabbi.

Life in the Spirit seminars: These are often given in both Protestant and Catholic churches as part of the charismatic renewal. They are tremendous faith-builders and life-changers. Ask about these seminars in your local church or parish.

The Cursillo movement: This is similar to Marriage Encounter but the participants are individuals rather than couples. The Cursillo movement is predominantly Catholic but is also open to non-Catholics. You can find out about the movement from your priest or minister.

Especially for Women

Catalyst (National Headquarters: 14 East Sixtieth Street, New York, N.Y. 10022; telephone: [212] 759–9700).

A national nonprofit organization dedicated to expanding career and family options for women. They have a staff of thirty full-time professionals and long-standing contacts in the corporate and professional communities. Catalyst's current priorities include addressing the needs of the undergraduate woman, the upwardly mobile woman and the two-career family.

The American Woman's Economic Development Corporation (Headquarters: 60 East Forty-second Street, New York, N.Y. 10165; telephone: [800] 222–AWED, or in New York City: 692–9100).

AWED is a federally funded organization providing business training and technical assistance to women since 1977. For women in business who need help immediately there is a hotline. A volunteer will provide ten minutes of toll-free counseling on a single question for a fee of five dollars.

Wider Opportunities for Woman, Inc. (Headquarters: 1325 G Street, N.W., Lower level, Washington, D.C. 20005; telephone: [202] 638–3145).

WOW's primary goal is to achieve equal employment opportunities for women through equal access to jobs and training, equal incomes and an equitable workplace. WOW published the first national directory of women's employment programs, which has served as a resource to individual women, libraries, universities, researchers, employers and others interested in women's employment issues.

Women's Action Alliance, Inc. (370 Lexington Avenue, New York, N.Y. 10017; telephone: [212] 532–8330).

Women's Action Alliance publishes a book entitled *Women Helping Women, A State by State Directory of Services.* This book is organized alphabetically by state, and within each state there are up to eight different kinds of service organizations listed: battered women and rape victim services; career counseling services; displaced homemaker programs; Planned Parenthood clinics; women's centers; women's commissions; and women's health services.

Problem Solving Organizations
Alcoholics Anonymous
Al-Anon
Overeaters Anonymous
Weight Watchers
YWCA

All these are national organizations and can be located through the phone book in your city.

QUESTIONNAIRE

We want to know about you. Please use as much space as you need to answer the following questions. Write on the back of the paper or take extra sheets of paper.

1. How old are you? _____

2. How long have you been married? _____

3. Is this your first marriage? _____

4. Is this your husband's first marriage? _____

5. Were you and your husband childhood sweethearts? _____

6. Did you have a happy childhood? _____

   _____

   _____

7. Why did you marry your husband? _____

   _____

   _____

8. How do you rate your marriage now? _____

   _____

   _____

9. What is your husband's profession? _____

10. How do you feel about your husband's profession? _____

_____

_____

11. Is your husband interested in your concerns? _____

_____

_____

12. Is your husband often away from home? _____

_____

13. How do you feel about this? _____

_____

_____

14. How much time do you and your husband have to yourselves as a couple? _____

_____

_____

15. Is this enough time together? _____

_____

_____

16. Please complete this sentence: "What I love most about my husband is _____

_____

_____

_____

17. Please complete this sentence: "I really get angry (or hurt, or frustrated) when my husband _____

_____

_____

18. What good effects has your husband's success had on your marriage? _____

_____

_____

_____

19. Has his success had any bad effects on your marriage? What are they? _____

_____

_____

20. Have you ever considered leaving your husband? If so, why? _____

_____

_____

21. If the answer to #20 was yes, why didn't you leave him? ___

_____

_____

This section concerns your children. If you do not have children, please skip ahead to question #32.

22. How many children do you have? _____

23. What are their ages? _____

24. Does (or did, if your children are now grown) your husband spend enough time with your children? _____

25. Does (or did) he wish he could spend more time with them? _____

26. When he is with the children, do (did) you find that his role is Santa Claus and yours a disciplinarian? _____

   _____

   _____

27. How does (did) he justify his time away from the children?

   _____

   _____

28. Have you had any serious problems with your children that you feel were caused by your husband's work or success? _____

   _____

   _____

29. What kind of sacrifices has your family had to make for your husband's career? _____

   _____

   _____

30. Do you think your son(s) would like to follow in their father's footsteps? How has his success affected them? _____

_____

_____

31. Would you want your daughter to marry an ambitious and successful man? Why or why not? _____

_____

_____

32. Before you married, what did you plan to do with your life? _____

_____

_____

_____

33. Do you have a career? _____

_____

_____

34. How does your husband feel about your career? _____

_____

_____

35. If you had to give up your career to foster his, how would you feel? _____

_____

_____

_____

36. Do you think that your career or career aspirations are a plus or a minus in your marriage? Please explain. _____

_____

_____

37. If you do volunteer work rather than pursue a career, please tell us about it. _____

_____

_____

38. We are interested in "support systems" for women: extended family, close friends, professional or social organizations. Please tell us about yours. _____

_____

_____

39. Do you have many good friends, the kind you could call in the middle of the night in an emergency? Are these long-term friends (ten years or more)? _____

_____

_____

40. Do you feel that you have outgrown some of your old friends? Is this all related to your husband's success? _____

_____

_____

41. Do you find, in making new friends, that you have to reach out more to people than you would if your husband weren't so successful? _____

_____

_____

42. Do you agree with this statement: "It's lonely at the top"? Why or why not? _____

_____

_____

43. Have you moved often in your married life? How often? _____

_____

44. Have frequent moves presented a problem? Why or why not? _____

_____

_____

45. Does your husband's position demand an official social life (business or professional entertaining)? Is this enjoyable or difficult for you? _____

_____

_____

46. Have you or your husband ever been criticized by strangers or the media? How do you feel about being in the public eye?

_____

_____

47. Are other women attracted to your husband because of his position? How do you handle this? _____

_____

_____

48. Do you agree with the statement: "Life at the top is disillusioning"? Why or why not? _____

_____

_____

49. If someone asked you who *you* were, what would you answer?

_____

_____

_____

50. If your husband left you tomorrow, what would you do? _____

_____

_____

51. Have you ever been, or are you now, envious of your husband's success? _____

_____

_____

52. Is he ever jealous of you? Why? _____

_____

_____

53. To what degree are you concerned by what others think of you? Do you have to be more careful in this respect because of your husband's position? _____

_____

_____

_____

54. Has your health been affected by the pressures of your husband's work? Please explain: _____

_____

_____

55. Has his health been affected by the pressures of his work? In what way? _____

_____

_____

56. Has the pressure of his work affected your sex life? To what extent? _____

_____

_____

57. Have you ever felt "burned out," unable to cope with your life? What happened when you felt this way? _____

_____

_____

_____

58. How did you keep going after this feeling? Where do you get your strength from? _____

_____ _____

_____

59. Do you feel that you have a strong sense of your own identity?

_____

_____

_____

_____

60. To what degree do you consider your identity linked to your spouse? _____

_____

_____

61. Would you tell a younger wife, leading a similar life, to "be yourself"? What does this phrase mean to you? _____

_____

_____

62. Do you feel that you and your husband are a team? Do you share outside interests? _____

_____

_____

_____

63. What are the rewards of being married to a successful man? _____

_____

_____

_____

64. Are the rewards worth the sacrifices? _____

_____

_____

_____

65. We are interested in compiling a list of resources for wives in your position. Could you recommend any books, organizations, techniques, attitudes or supports which could be of help to other "wives at the top"? _____

_____

_____

_____

_____

Thank you so much for taking the time to fill out this question-naire!

INDEX